INTERMEDIATE 2

ART & DESIGN
2008-2011

Publisher's Note

We are delighted to bring you the 2011 Past Papers and you will see that we have changed the format from previous editions. As part of our environmental awareness strategy, we have attempted to make these new editions as sustainable as possible.

To do this, we have printed on white paper and bound the answer sections into the book. This not only allows us to use significantly less paper but we are also, for the first time, able to source all the materials from sustainable sources.

We hope you like the new editions and by purchasing this product, you are not only supporting an independent Scottish publishing company but you are also, in the International Year of Forests, not contributing to the destruction of the world's forests.

Thank you for your support and please see the following websites for more information to support the above statement –

www.fsc-uk.org

www.loveforests.com

© Scottish Qualifications Authority
All rights reserved. Copying prohibited. No part of this publication may be reproduced, stored in a retrieval system, or transmitted in any form or by any means, electronic, mechanical, photocopying, recording or otherwise.

First exam published in 2008.
Published by Bright Red Publishing Ltd, 6 Stafford Street, Edinburgh EH3 7AU
tel: 0131 220 5804 fax: 0131 220 6710 info@brightredpublishing.co.uk www.brightredpublishing.co.uk

ISBN 978-1-84948-193-9

A CIP Catalogue record for this book is available from the British Library.

Bright Red Publishing is grateful to the copyright holders, as credited on the final page of the Question Section, for permission to use their material. Every effort has been made to trace the copyright holders and to obtain their permission for the use of copyright material. Bright Red Publishing will be happy to receive information allowing us to rectify any error or omission in future editions.

[BLANK PAGE]

X223/201

NATIONAL QUALIFICATIONS 2008	TUESDAY, 3 JUNE 1.00 PM – 2.00 PM	ART AND DESIGN INTERMEDIATE 2

There are **two** sections to this paper, Section 1—Art Studies; and Section 2—Design Studies.

Each section is worth 20 marks.

Candidates should attempt questions as follows:

In SECTION 1 answer **ONE full question** (parts (*a*) **and** (*b*))

and

In SECTION 2 answer **ONE full question** (parts (*a*) **and** (*b*)).

You may use sketches to illustrate your answers.

SECTION 1—ART STUDIES

Instructions

Read your selected question and notes on the illustration carefully.

Answer **ONE full question** from this section: parts **(a)** and **(b)**.

Portrait of the Journalist Sylvia Von Harden (1926) by Otto Dix,
oil and tempera on wood (120 × 88 cm)

Marks

1. Portraiture

(a) In your opinion, how well does the artist use *colour*, *shape* and *composition* to show the character of his model? **10**

(b) Compare and contrast **two** portraits by any **two** artists. Explain the main differences in the portraits. How successful are they, in your opinion? **10**

SECTION 1—ART STUDIES (continued)

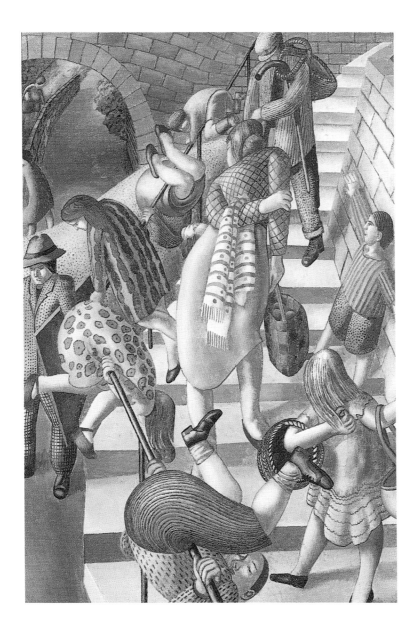

The Glen, Port Glasgow (1952) by Sir Stanley Spencer,
oil on canvas (76·2 × 50·9 cm)

Marks

2. Figure Composition

(a) How well does the artist use any **three** of the following to make this scene of children at play appealing to the viewer?

> *line*   *colour*   *shape*   *pattern*   *tone*

Justify your opinion.

10

(b) Discuss **two** figure compositions by any **two** artists. Explain why, in your opinion, they are successful. Refer to each artist's approach to figure composition.

10

[Turn over

SECTION 1—ART STUDIES (continued)

Still Life: Autumn Fashion (1978) by Patrick Caulfield,
acrylic on canvas (61 × 76.2 cm)

Marks

3. Still Life

(*a*) Give your opinion of this approach to still life. Comment on the use of *visual elements* and *composition*. Do you think this is a successful still life? Give your reasons.   **10**

(*b*) Discuss **two** examples of still life by any **two** artists. Explain why, in your opinion, they are good examples of still life.   **10**

SECTION 1—ART STUDIES (continued)

The Storm (1890) by William McTaggart,
oil on canvas (122 × 183 cm)

Marks

4. Natural Environment

(*a*) In your opinion, how well does the artist use *tone*, *colour* and *media* to show the violent forces of nature in this work?

10

(*b*) Compare **two** works by **two** different artists who base their work on the natural environment. Explain any differences in their approaches, use of media and visual elements. Give your opinion on the success of your chosen examples.

10

[Turn over

SECTION 1—ART STUDIES (continued)

Place du Tertre (1911) by Maurice Utrillo,
oil on canvas (50·2 × 73 cm)

Marks

5. Built Environment

(*a*) How well, in your opinion, does the artist's use of media and visual elements contribute to the success of this quiet street scene?   **10**

(*b*) Compare **two** works by **two** different artists who use or create built environment in their work. Comment on the success of the methods that they use. Give your opinion of the works.   **10**

SECTION 1—ART STUDIES (continued)

The Great Red Dragon and the Woman Clothed in Sun (1806–1809) by William Blake,
watercolour on paper (42 × 34·3 cm)

Marks

6. **Fantasy and Imagination**

(a) In your opinion, how well are *light*, *composition* and *colour* used to give a sense   **10**
of threat and fear in this work?

(b) Compare and contrast **two** works by **two** artists who have different
approaches to creating fantasy and imagination in their work. Which do you   **10**
prefer and why?

[Turn over

SECTION 2—DESIGN STUDIES

Instructions

Read your selected question and notes on the illustration carefully.

Answer **ONE full question** from this section: parts **(a)** and **(b)**.

Tekken 4, cover design for Sony PlayStation 2 game (1997)

Marks

7.   Graphic Design

(*a*)   How well has the designer created a cover design for an exciting computer game? Refer to the following:

- imagery;

- lettering;   **10**

- layout.

(*b*)   Select **two** graphic designs by different designers. Explain the methods used   **10**
to achieve originality and visual impact.

SECTION 2—DESIGN STUDIES (continued)

Teapot designed by Marianne Brandt (1924).
Materials: silver with hardwood handle.

Marks

8. Product Design

(a)   In your opinion, how well has the designer combined *style, function* and *use of*   **10**
materials in this teapot?

(b)   Compare and contrast **two** products by different designers. Refer to any **two**
of the following:

- style;

- use of materials;

- function;   **10**

- methods of construction.

[Turn over

SECTION 2—DESIGN STUDIES (continued)

Rogano Restaurant, designed by Weddell and Inglis (1937)

Marks

9. Interior Design

(a) In your opinion, how well has the designer created a suitable interior for an upmarket restaurant? Refer to *use of space*, *colour* and *furniture and fittings*.   **10**

(b) Compare and contrast **two** examples of interior design by different designers. Refer to **two** of the following:

- style;

- use of space;

- use of lighting;

- use of materials.   **10**

SECTION 2—DESIGN STUDIES (continued)

The Falkirk Wheel, designed by RMJM architects (2002).

The design enables boats to be raised and lowered between the high level canal and the lower canal.

Marks

10. Environmental/Architectural Design

(*a*) In your opinion, how successful is this design? Refer to *form*, *function* and *scale*.   **10**

(*b*) Explain the importance of *fitness for purpose* and *style* in **two** examples of environmental or architectural design by different designers.   **10**

[Turn over

SECTION 2—DESIGN STUDIES (continued)

Tiara and Brooch, designed for the Empress Eugenie by Gabriel Lemonnier (1853).
Materials: gold, pearls and diamonds.

Marks

11. Jewellery Design

(a)   Give your opinion on the main *function* of these jewellery pieces, with reference to *style*, *use of materials* and *target market*.   **10**

(b)   Compare and contrast **two** designs by different jewellery designers, with reference to *style* and *use of materials*.   **10**

SECTION 2—DESIGN STUDIES (continued)

Gentleman's outfit by unknown French designer (circa 1800)

Marks

12. Textile/Fashion Design

(a) Discuss this outfit with reference to *style*, *function* and *wearability*. How does it differ from formal dress for men today?   **10**

(b) Select **two** examples of fashion or textile design by different designers. Identify the most important aspects of their work with reference to *style* and *target market*.   **10**

[END OF QUESTION PAPER]

[BLANK PAGE]

[BLANK PAGE]

X223/201

NATIONAL
QUALIFICATIONS
2009

FRIDAY, 5 JUNE
1.00 PM – 2.00 PM

ART AND DESIGN
INTERMEDIATE 2

There are **two** sections to this paper, Section 1—Art Studies; and Section 2—Design Studies.

Each section is worth 20 marks.

Candidates should attempt questions as follows:

In SECTION 1 answer **ONE full question** (parts (*a*) **and** (*b*))

and

In SECTION 2 answer **ONE full question** (parts (*a*) **and** (*b*)).

You may use sketches to illustrate your answers.

XSQA

SECTION 1—ART STUDIES

Instructions

Read your selected question and notes on the illustration carefully.

Answer **ONE full question** from this section: parts **(a)** and **(b)**.

Self Portrait by Stephen Conroy (2005)
oil on canvas (207 × 147 cm)

Marks

1. Portraiture

(a) How well does the artist use *tone*, *shape* and *composition* to show strong
    emotion in this portrait?   **10**

(b) Compare and contrast approaches to portraiture in **two** works by different
    artists. Which do you prefer and why?   **10**

SECTION 1—ART STUDIES (continued)

Tourists II by Duane Hanson (1988) the figures are lifesize.
This sculpture is made of autobody filler, fibreglass and mixed media
with real clothes and accessories.

Marks

2. Figure Composition

(a) Give your opinion of this sculpture. Refer to the *choice of subject*, *pose* and *the media* used by the artist to create the work. **10**

(b) Discuss **two** figure compositions by different artists. Explain why, in your opinion, they are successful. Refer to each artist's approach to figure composition. **10**

[Turn over

SECTION 1—ART STUDIES (continued)

Still Life by Richard Diebenkorn (1967)
black ink, Conté crayon, charcoal and ballpoint pen on paper (35·2 × 42·5 cm)

Marks

3.   Still Life

(a)   Give your opinion on the artist's use of *media, composition* and *choice of subject matter* in this still life. Do you think this is a successful still life? Give your reasons.   **10**

(b)   Discuss **two** examples of still life by different artists. Contrast their use of media and visual elements. Explain why, in your opinion, they are good examples of still life.   **10**

SECTION 1—ART STUDIES (continued)

Glencoe by Horatio McCulloch (1864)
oil on canvas (110 × 183 cm)

Marks

4. Natural Environment

(*a*) How well does the artist use *tone*, *colour* and *composition* to show the mood and atmosphere of this highland scene?   **10**

(*b*) Compare **two** works by different artists who are influenced by the natural environment. Explain why you think they are successful examples of work in this theme.   **10**

[Turn over

SECTION 1—ART STUDIES (continued)

London Bridge by Andre Derain (1906)
oil on canvas (66 × 99 cm)

Marks

5. Built Environment

(a) How well, in your opinion, does the artist's use of *media, colour* and *shape* contribute to the success of this busy river scene?   **10**

(b) Comment on the media and methods used in **two** artworks by different artists who work in the theme of built environment. State why you think they are good examples of work in this theme.   **10**

SECTION 1—ART STUDIES (continued)

The Beached Margin by Edward Wadsworth (1937)
tempera paint on linen (71 × 101 cm)

Marks

6. Fantasy and Imagination

(*a*) In your opinion, how well does the artist create a sense of fantasy and imagination in this work? Refer to the use of *visual elements* and *composition*.   **10**

(*b*) Discuss the methods and approaches used in **two** works by different artists to create fantasy and imagination.   **10**

[Turn over

SECTION 2—DESIGN STUDIES

Instructions

Read your selected question and notes on the illustration carefully.

Answer **ONE full question** from this section: parts **(a)** and **(b)**.

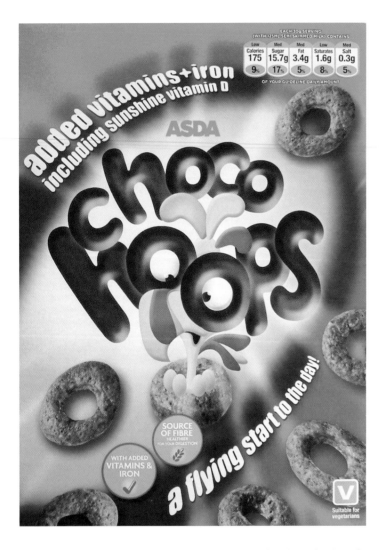 

Breakfast cereal packaging design for ASDA (2007)

Marks

7.   Graphic Design

(a)   What target market is this packaging design aimed at?   Refer to use of *imagery*, *lettering* and *colour*.   Do you think it is successful?   **10**

(b)   Compare **two** graphic designs by different designers.   Identify and discuss the methods used to create effective designs with visual impact.   **10**

SECTION 2—DESIGN STUDIES (continued)

Gramophone designed for Pathé (1908), height 67 cm.

This early music system is operated by a clockwork mechanism which requires the user to wind up the handle.

Marks

8. Product Design

(*a*) How does this gramophone compare to today's products for playing music? Refer to *appearance* and *function*.   **10**

(*b*) Select **two** products by different designers. Compare the methods used by the designers to create products which are functional and visually appealing to the consumer.   **10**

[Turn over

SECTION 2—DESIGN STUDIES (continued)

Barajas Airport Terminal, Madrid, designed by Richard Rodgers Partnership (2006).
Materials: aluminium, glass, wood, polished stone and tempered glass floor tiles.

Marks

9. Interior Design

(a) How well have the designers of this airport terminal created a stylish interior?
Refer to *structure*, *use of space* and *materials*.   **10**

(b) Compare **two** interiors by different designers. With reference to the key
design issues, discuss how the designers have produced aesthetically pleasing
spaces which meet the needs of the users.   **10**

SECTION 2—DESIGN STUDIES (continued)

The Opera House, Paris, designed by Charles Garnier (1861–1875)

Marks

10. Environmental/Architectural Design

(*a*) How well has the architect designed a building which has a sense of importance? Refer to *form*, *decoration* and *scale*.

10

(*b*) Compare **two** examples of environmental/architectural design. Comment on the different approaches to style, materials and purpose.

10

[Turn over

SECTION 2—DESIGN STUDIES (continued)

Wrist watch designed by Boucheron (1942).
Materials: gold set with diamonds and sapphires.

Marks

11. Jewellery Design

(*a*) What is your opinion of this piece of jewellery? Refer to *style*, *materials* and *fitness for purpose*.

10

(*b*) Select **two** examples of jewellery by different designers. Compare the different sources of inspiration and techniques used to produce visually exciting pieces of jewellery.

10

SECTION 2—DESIGN STUDIES (continued)

Photo by Bishin Jumonji © 1971
as seen in *The Art of Zandra Rhodes*.

Dinosaur coat and hat designed by Zandra Rhodes (1971).
Materials: wool felt, printed silk lining and appliqué silk flowers.

Marks

12. Textile/Fashion Design

(*a*)   How successful is this outfit? Refer to *sources of inspiration*, *form* and *detail*.   **10**

(*b*)   Select **two** examples of work by different textile or fashion designers. Explain how these examples are typical of each designer's individual style. Refer to their sources of inspiration and use of materials.   **10**

[END OF QUESTION PAPER]

[BLANK PAGE]

2010

[BLANK PAGE]

X223/201

NATIONAL QUALIFICATIONS 2010	FRIDAY, 4 JUNE 1.00 PM – 2.00 PM	ART AND DESIGN INTERMEDIATE 2

There are **two** sections to this paper, Section 1—Art Studies; and Section 2—Design Studies.

Each section is worth 20 marks.

Candidates should attempt questions as follows:

In SECTION 1 answer **ONE full question** (parts (*a*) **and** (*b*))

and

In SECTION 2 answer **ONE full question** (parts (*a*) **and** (*b*)).

You may use sketches to illustrate your answers.

SECTION 1—ART STUDIES

Instructions

Read your selected question and notes on the illustration carefully.

Answer **ONE full question** from this section: parts **(a)** and **(b)**.

The Desperate Man by Gustave Courbet (1844–45)
oil on canvas (45 × 55 cm)

Marks

1. Portraiture

(a) How well does the artist use *pose*, *tone* and *colour* to create this attention-grabbing self portrait? What is the artist trying to communicate to us in this self-portrait?   **10**

(b) Discuss **two** portraits by **two** different artists. Comment on their use of the visual elements and explain why these works are good examples of portraiture.   **10**

SECTION 1—ART STUDIES (continued)

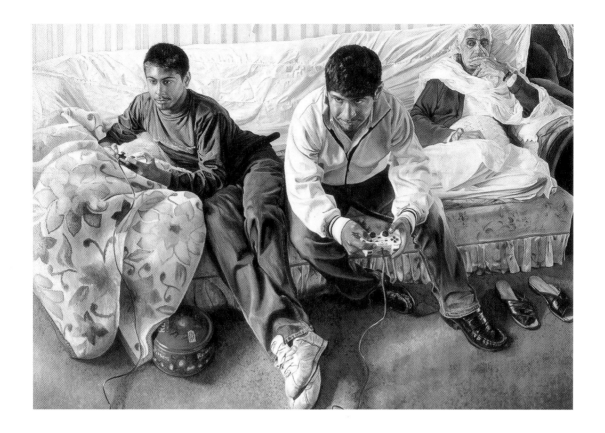

Gran Turismo[1] by Megan Davies (2005)
oil on canvas (125 × 172 cm)

[1]*Gran Turismo* is a computer game.

Marks

2. Figure Composition

(*a*) In your opinion, how well does the artist respond to this everyday family situation? Comment on the use of *colour*, *light* and *composition*.   **10**

(*b*) Discuss **two** figure compositions by any **two** artists. Explain why, in your opinion, they are successful. Refer to each artist's approach to technique and style.   **10**

[Turn over

SECTION 1—ART STUDIES (continued)

Maple and Chocolate by Ralph Goings (2004)
oil on canvas (23 × 30·5 cm)

Marks

3. **Still Life**

(a) Comment on the artist's choice of *subject matter* and use of visual elements. What is your opinion of this painting?   **10**

(b) Compare and contrast **two** still lifes by **two** different artists. Explain why, in your opinion, they are good examples of still life. Discuss their different styles and techniques.   **10**

SECTION 1—ART STUDIES (continued)

Frosty Morning, Trow Hill by Anne Redpath (1935)
oil on plywood (78 × 90 cm)

Marks

4.   Natural Environment

(*a*)   In your opinion, how well has the artist shown a frosty morning scene? Refer to *colour*, *mood* and *technique*.

10

(*b*)   The natural environment has inspired many artists. Discuss **two** examples by **two** different artists. Explain why, in your opinion, they are good responses to this theme.

10

[Turn over

SECTION 1—ART STUDIES (continued)

Street Study outside a School by The Boyle Family (1988)
cast and painted fibreglass (182·5 × 182·5 × 15–30 cm)

This 3-D art work was made by taking a cast of a section of ground.

Fibreglass is a lightweight material which can be used to create 3-D forms.

Marks

5. Built Environment

(a) Give your opinion of this response to the built environment. Refer to the use of *scale*, *composition* and *texture*.   **10**

(b) Compare and contrast **two** works by **two** different artists who use the theme of the built environment. Comment on the methods used. Give your opinion of the success of these works.   **10**

SECTION 1—ART STUDIES (continued)

Life from *Death Life Hope Fear* by Gilbert and George (1984)
mixed media (422 × 250 cm)

Marks

6. Fantasy and Imagination

(a) Give your opinion of this photographic work. Comment on these artists' use of *colour*, *scale* and *composition*. **10**

(b) Compare **two** works by **two** different artists who base their work on fantasy and imagination. Explain the differences in their approaches. Give your opinion of your chosen examples. **10**

[Turn over

SECTION 2—DESIGN STUDIES

Instructions

Read your selected question and notes on the illustration carefully.

Answer **ONE full question** from this section: parts **(a)** and **(b)**.

Vertigo–film poster designed by Saul Bass (1958)

The word Vertigo means: dizziness, light headedness

Marks

7.   Graphic Design

(a)   What does this poster communicate to you about the film? Refer to the use of
lettering, *colour* and *imagery*.   **10**

(b)   Select **two** examples of work by different graphic designers. Compare the
techniques used to create memorable graphic designs.   **10**

SECTION 2—DESIGN STUDIES (continued)

Lego–plastic construction toy, designed by Ole Kirk and Godtfred Christiansen (1958)

Interlocking building bricks.

Marks

8. Product Design

(a) Why do you think this product is still being sold successfully today? Refer to *fitness for purpose*, *use of materials* and *target market*.   **10**

(b) Select **two** products by different designers. Comment on how the designers have created successful designs referring to **three** of the following:

- style;
- function;
- use of materials;
- sources of inspiration;
- use of technology;
- target market.   **10**

[Turn over

SECTION 2—DESIGN STUDIES (continued)

Cookery classroom, Scotland Street School, designed by Charles Rennie Mackintosh (1906)

Marks

9. Interior Design

(a) How does this design compare with contemporary classrooms used for the teaching of food preparation? Refer to *decoration*, *furnishings* and *use of space*.   **10**

(b) Select **two** interior designs by different designers. Explain their individual approaches to creating new and exciting interior spaces.   **10**

SECTION 2—DESIGN STUDIES (continued)

Trellick Tower, London, designed by Erno Goldfinger (1972)
Materials: reinforced concrete and glass.

Marks

10. Environmental/Architectural Design

(a) In your opinion, how successful is this building in providing housing for a large number of families in an inner city environment? Refer to *form*, *function* and *scale*. **10**

(b) Select **two** examples of environmental/architectural design by different designers. Discuss how *style*, *function* and *materials* have contributed to the success of each design. **10**

[Turn over

SECTION 2—DESIGN STUDIES (continued)

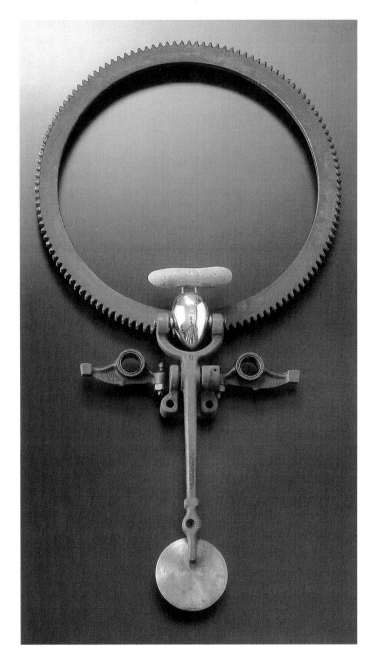

Regenerat–assembled pendant by Wahei Ikezawa (1994).
Materials: stone; iron; brass (60 × 30 cm).

Marks

11. Jewellery Design

(a) Discuss how the designer has used *found materials* to create this piece of statement jewellery. In your opinion, is it a successful design in terms of *style* and *wearability*?

10

(b) Select **two** pieces of jewellery by different designers. Explain how they have created imaginative designs referring to their *sources of inspiration, materials* and *working methods.*

10

SECTION 2—DESIGN STUDIES (continued)

[Unfortunately, due to copyright restrictions, we are unable to
reproduce this image.]

Hand-knit Jacket and Sweater, Fringed Skirt by [. . .] (1983)

Marks

12. Textile/Fashion Design

(a) In your view, how successfully were each of the following considered by the designer:

• aesthetics;

• target market;

• use of materials?   **10**

(b) Discuss the work of **two** textile or fashion designers. Identify the most important features of their designs.   **10**

[BLANK PAGE]

[BLANK PAGE]

X223/201

NATIONAL
QUALIFICATIONS
2011

THURSDAY, 2 JUNE
1.00 PM – 2.00 PM

ART AND DESIGN
INTERMEDIATE 2

There are **two** sections to this paper, Section 1—Art Studies; and Section 2—Design Studies.

Each section is worth 20 marks.

Candidates should attempt questions as follows:

In SECTION 1 answer **ONE full question** (parts (*a*) **and** (*b*))

and

In SECTION 2 answer **ONE full question** (parts (*a*) **and** (*b*)).

You may use sketches to illustrate your answers.

SECTION 1—ART STUDIES

Instructions

Read your selected question and notes on the illustration carefully.

Answer **ONE full question** from this section: parts **(a)** and **(b)**.

My Mother, Bolton Abbey, Yorkshire, Nov. 1982
photographic collage (120·7 × 69·9 cm)

Marks

1. Portraiture

(a) How well does the artist use *the photographic technique* and *viewpoint* to create this interesting portrait? What is the artist trying to communicate to us in this composition?   **10**

(b) Compare the methods and approaches used in **two** works by different artists to create successful portraits.   **10**

SECTION 1—ART STUDIES (continued)

The Tennis Party by John Lavery (1885)
oil on canvas (77 × 183 cm)

Marks

2. **Figure Composition**

(*a*)   In your opinion, what makes this a successful figure composition?

Comment on the artist's use of *tone, colour* and *pose*.   **10**

(*b*)   Select **two** figure compositions by different artists. Contrast their use of media and visual elements. Explain in your own opinion why they are good examples of figure composition.   **10**

[Turn over

SECTION 1—ART STUDIES (continued)

Table by a Window by Jean Metzinger (1917)
oil on canvas (81·3 × 65·1 cm)

Marks

3. Still Life

(a) Comment on the artist's use of *shape*, *colour* and *pattern* in this work.

What is your opinion of this composition?   **10**

(b) Comment on the subject matter and methods used in **two** artworks by different artists who work in the area of still life. State why you think they are successful examples.   **10**

SECTION 1—ART STUDIES (continued)

Due to copyright restrictions, the image has been removed. It can be viewed at: http://www.toledomuseum.org/ by clicking the link to 'Our Collection'. Next, in the 'Quick Search' box on the left-hand side please type in 'Andrew Wyeth', then click on the 'Object' link to view the image

The Hunter by Andrew Wyeth (1943)
tempera paint on panel (83·8 × 86·4 cm)

Marks

4. Natural Environment

(*a*) How well has the artist's choice of viewpoint contributed to the mood and atmosphere of this hunting scene? Comment on the artist's use of *colour* and *shape*.

10

(*b*) The natural environment has inspired many artists. Compare **two** examples by different artists. Explain why, in your opinion, these are good responses to this theme.

10

[Turn over

SECTION 1—ART STUDIES (continued)

Cabina[1] *NY* by Jose Luis Corella (2006)
oil on board (117 × 98 cm)

[1]*Cabina* means telephone box.

Marks

5. Built Environment

(*a*)   Give your opinion of this artist's choice of subject matter in this response to the built environment. Refer to *colour*, *texture* and *composition*.   **10**

(*b*)   Compare **two** works by different artists who use the theme of the built environment. Comment on the methods used. Give your opinion of the success of these works.   **10**

SECTION 1—ART STUDIES (continued)

Saint Bride by John Duncan (1913)
tempera paint on canvas (122·3 × 144·5 cm)

Marks

6. Fantasy and Imagination

(a) In your opinion, what kind of atmosphere has the artist created in this work? Refer to the use of *colour*, *pattern* and *imagery*.   **10**

(b) Compare and contrast approaches to fantasy and imagination in **two** works by different artists. Which do you prefer and why?   **10**

[Turn over

SECTION 2—DESIGN STUDIES

Instructions

Read your selected question and notes on the illustration carefully.

Answer **ONE full question** from this section: parts **(a)** and **(b)**.

Magazine cover designed by Aubrey Beardsley (1895)

Marks

7.   Graphic Design

(a)   Give your opinion on how this design compares with contemporary magazine
covers. Refer to *imagery*, *lettering* and *layout*.   **10**

(b)   Select **two** graphic designs by different designers. Compare how successful they
are in achieving visual impact and communication with a target audience.   **10**

SECTION 2—DESIGN STUDIES (continued)

Cross-section of car interior

Morris Mini-Minor designed by Sir Alec Issigonis (1959)

Marks

8. Product Design

(a) How well has the designer of this small, low cost car considered *fitness for purpose* and *style*? What *target market* would have found it appealing? **10**

(b) Select **two** products by different designers. Identify the key design issues considered and discuss each designer's approach to creating a successful product. **10**

SECTION 2—DESIGN STUDIES (continued)

Topshop store in New York designed by Dalziel and Pow (2009)

Marks

9. Interior Design

(a) In your opinion, how well have the designers created this high street store interior? How successfully do the *use of space* and *style* contribute to its consumer appeal?   **10**

(b) Select **two** interiors by different designers. Compare the methods used to create effective and attractive interior spaces.   **10**

SECTION 2—DESIGN STUDIES (continued)

Interior of lounge area

View of rear of Centre and
surrounding area

Maggie's Centre, Dundee, designed by Frank Gehry (2004)
Materials: stainless steel roof, reinforced concrete and wood.

Maggie's Centres are drop-in facilities for people affected by cancer.

Marks

10. Environmental/Architectural Design

(a)   Give your opinion on the design of this building. Refer to *structure* and *use of materials*. What do you think could have been the designer's *source of inspiration*?   **10**

(b)   Compare **two** successful examples of environmental/architectural design by different designers. Refer to important design issues in your answer.   **10**

SECTION 2—DESIGN STUDIES (continued)

 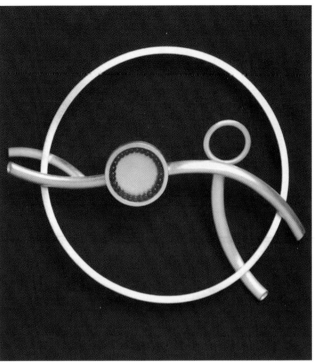

Brooches from the *Artery* series designed by Dorothy Hogg (2005)
Materials: silver and coral
diameter: 11 cm

Dorothy Hogg's work springs from her experience of life and change. Her work in the Artery Series is concerned with ideas of flow within and through matter. The pieces are meticulously constructed in sheet silver to create hollow forms that have visual weight without the expected physical density, while the colour red is used for its powerful symbolic value.   (*Photographer: John K. McGregor*)

Marks

11. Jewellery Design

(a) Give your opinion of this designer's use of parts of the human body as a *source of inspiration*. Refer to *style* in your answer. Who might find these pieces attractive to buy?   **10**

(b) Select **two** examples of work by different jewellery designers. Compare the designers' influences and the techniques used to make visually appealing designs.   **10**

SECTION 2—DESIGN STUDIES (continued)

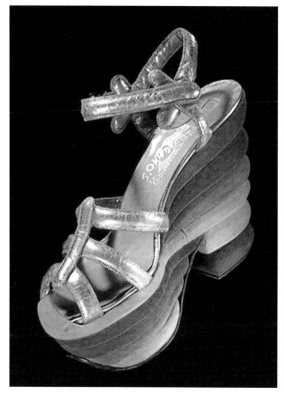 

Sandal designed by Salvatore Ferragamo (1938)
Materials: leather, suede and cork with metal buckle.

Marks

12. Textile/Fashion Design

(a) How well did the designer create a shoe which makes a fashion statement? Refer to *form* and *practicality*. Who might have worn these shoes?   **10**

(b) Discuss **two** examples of textile/fashion by different designers.

With reference to style and use of materials, compare how the designs appeal to specific target markets.   **10**

[END OF QUESTION PAPER]

[BLANK PAGE]

Acknowledgements

Permission has been sought from all relevant copyright holders and Bright Red Publishing is grateful for the use of the following:

Portrait of Sylvia Von Harden by Otto Dix © DACS 2011/Agence Photographique (2008 page 2);

The painting 'The Glen, Port Glasgow' by Sir Stanley Spencer © The Estate of Stanley Spencer. All Rights Reserved DACS, 2011 (2008 page 3);

The painting 'Still Life – Autumn Fashion' by Patrick Caulfield © The Estate of Patrick Caulfield. All Rights Reserved DACS, 2011 (2008 page 4);

The painting 'The Storm' by William McTaggart © Dundee City Council – Arts and Heritage. Licensor www.scran.ac.uk (2008 page 5);

The painting 'La Place du Tertre' by Maurice Utrillo © ADAGP, Paris and DACS, London 2011. Digital image © Tate, London 2010 (2008 page 6);

The painting 'The Great Red Dragon and the Woman Clothed in Sun' by William Blake. Reproduced by permission of Brooklyn Museum (2008 page 7);

Picture of Tekken 4, cover design for Sony Playstation 2 game (1997) © Namco/Sony Computer Entertainment Inc (2008 page 8);

A picture of a Teapot designed by Marianne Brandt © DACS 2011/Bauhaus-Archiv Berlin (2008 page 9);

Two photographs of Rogano Restaurant © University of Strathclyde. Licensor www.scran.ac.uk (2008 page 10);

A picture of a Tiara and Brooch, designed for the Empress Eugenie by Gabriel Lemonnier (1853), courtesy of Sotheby's (2008 page 12);

A picture of Her Imperial and Royal Highness Princess Margarete von Thurn und Taxis (Fürst Thurn und Taxis Zentralarchiv-Fotosammlung) (2008 page 12);

Two pictures of a gentleman's outfit © V&A Images/Victoria and Albert Museum (2008 page 13);

The painting 'Self Portrait' by Stephen Conroy © Stephen Conroy UK/Culture and Sport Glasgow (Museums) (2009 page 2);

The sculpture 'Tourists II' by Duane Hanson © Estate of Duane Hanson/Licensed by VAGA, New York, NY (2009 page 3);

The painting 'Still Life' by Richard Diebenkorn (1967). Image courtesy of the Board of Trustees, National Gallery of Art, Washington © The Richard Diebenkorn Foundation (2009 page 4);

The painting 'Glencoe' by Horatio McCulloch © Glasgow Museums. Licensor www.scran.ac.uk (2009 page 5);

The painting 'London Bridge' by André Derain © ADAGP, Paris and DACS, London 2011. Digital image © (2011) The Museum of Modern Art, NewYork/Scala, Florence (2009 page 6);

The painting 'The Beached Margin' by Edward Wadsworth © Tate, London 2010 (2009 page 7);

Breakfast cereal packaging for ASDA (2007) © ASDA (2009 page 8);

Gramophone designed for Pathé (1908) © The Robert Opie Collection (2009 page 9);

Three photographs of 'Barajas Airport Terminal, Madrid' by Manuel Renau © Aena (2009 page 10);

The photograph 'The Opera House, Paris' by Delagarde and Moatti © Jean-Pierre Delagarde & Jacques Moatti (2009 page 11);

A photograph of a wrist watch designed by Boucheron (1942) © Boucheron (2009 page 12);

A photograph of a Dinosaur coat and hat designed by Zandra Rhodes (1971) © Bishin Jumonji (left) and a photograph of a Dinosaur coat © Zandra Rhodes (right) (2009 page 13);

'The Desperate Man' by Gustave Courbet. Private Collection by courtesy of BNP Paribas Art Advisory (2010 page 2);

The painting 'Gran Turismo' by Megan Davies (2005) © Megan Davies (2010 page 3);

The painting 'Maple and Chocolate' by Ralph Goings (2004) © Ralph Goings (2010 page 4);

The painting 'Frosty Morning, Trow Hill' by Anne Redpath (1935) © Royal Scottish Academy (2010 page 5);

'Street Study outside a School' © Boyle Family. All rights reserved, DACS 2011 (2010 page 6);

'Life' from 'Death Life Hope Fear' 1984 (422 x 250 cm) © Gilbert & George (2010 page 7);

The poster 'Vertigo' designed by Saul Bass. Courtesy of Universal Studios Licensing LLC (2010 page 8);

A picture of Lego © Lego Group Ltd (2010 page 9);

Two photographs of a cookery classroom from Scotland Street School, designed by Charles Rennie Mackintosh (1906) © Martin Smith (2010 page 10);

A photograph of Trellick Tower, London © Edifice www.edificephoto.com (2010 page 11);

A picture of Regenerat, an assembled pendant by Wahei Ikezawa (1994), taken from 'Design Source Book Jewellery' by David Watkins, published by New Holland Publishers (UK) Ltd (2010 page 12);

David Hockney 'My Mother, Bolton Abbey, Yorkshire, Nov. 1982' Photographic Collage, Edition of 20, 47½ x 27½ © David Hockney (2011 page 2);

'The Tennis Party' by John Lavery, taken from Aberdeen Art Gallery & Museums Collections. By courtesy of Felix Rosenstiel's Widow & Son Ltd., London on behalf of the Estate of Sir John Lavery (2011 page 3);

'Table by a Window' by Jean Metzinger © 2011. Image copyright The Metropolitan Museum of Art/Art Resource/Scala, Florence (2011 page 4);

'Cabina NY' by Jose Luis Corella © DACS 2011 (2011 page 6);

'Saint Bride' by John Duncan © Estate of John Duncan. All rights reserved, DACS 2011 (2011 page 7);

Poster for 'The Studio' by Aubrey Beardsley © Victoria and Albert Museum, London (2011 page 8);

Two photos from: http://commons.wikimedia.org/wiki/File:Mini_cross_section.jpg and http://commons.wikimedia.org/wiki/File:Morris_Mini-Minor_1959.jpg. Both licensed under the Creative Commons Attribution-ShareAlike 3.0 Unported Licence (CC BY-SA 3). Details can be viewed at: http://creativecommons.org/licenses/by-sa/3.0/deed.en (2011 page 9);

SQA INTERMEDIATE 2
ART & DESIGN 2008–2011

Overview

The Art and Design Studies Examination Component 2 - Question Paper has been set with the following principles in mind:

1. The examination set for Art and Design Studies at Intermediate 2 level should clearly articulate with the Higher level. The format of the Intermediate 2 examination paper is therefore similar to the Higher paper with respect to the reference materials used and the six headed questions in each of the two sections: Art Studies and Design Studies.

2. Intermediate 2 candidates are required to demonstrate knowledge and understanding of selected aspects of the visual arts and design and to formulate, explain and communicate personal opinions and conclusions. The format of the questions reflects this emphasis. Each question has two equally demanding parts. Parts (a) and (b) are designed to test the candidates' ability to respond critically to a range of visual arts imagery and design products and to form and substantiate judgements about identified aspects of art practice and design issues. The questions also require candidates to demonstrate knowledge and understanding gained through their Art and Design Studies as follows:

   Part (a)

   This part of the question requires candidates to give a descriptive response to a selected illustration from the supplied reference materials using appropriate terminology and making reference to identified aspects of Art and Design practice.

   Part (b)

   This part of the question requires candidates to make a personal critical response to identified visual elements and art practice in Section 1 of the paper and to identify visual aspects and design issues in Section 2 of the paper. Candidates are expected to substantiate reasons to support judgements and personal opinions expressed in their responses to this part of the question.

3. All questions are of equal demand. The questions should be suitable for candidates with a relatively detailed knowledge as well as those whose knowledge is more wide ranging.

4. It is important that candidates respond with answers, to part *(b)* of the question, that contain a depth of knowledge and understanding of their specialist area of the visual arts and design. In these instances, candidates will be well rewarded.

5. In Art Studies, questions where the term "artist" is used it should be interpreted in its broadest sense, covering painting, printmaking, photography, sculpture, installation, animation, film and video.

6. Similarly in the Design Studies questions, the term 'designer' should be inclusive of any form of design.

Art Studies

1. **Portraiture**
   (*a*) In responses to this part of the question, candidates will be given credit for well-justified personal opinions about the use of the visual elements of colour, shape and composition. This may include comment on the harsh exposure of the weaknesses of the model, the ruthless exaggeration and realism, brutal honesty and sense of caricature. The dominance of red providing emphasis for the figure may suggest to you that the personality of the model is linked to the colour.

   Candidates may link the idea of the sitter to the profession of journalism and give ideas about her character from your knowledge of this.

   Reference to the composition should refer to the placing of the figure in relation to the table and the dramatic positioning of the hands.

   Shape is important throughout all the parts of the painting and should be noted by reference to the artist's portrayal of the figure, the hands and table.

   To gain a very good mark in this part of the question, candidates must comment on each of the visual elements and draw straightforward conclusions about their effect on the depiction of the character of the sitter.

   Candidates may well use descriptive terms like angry, agitated etc to describe the character and you will be credited with well justified observations.

   (*b*) Any significant portraiture within the range period set for Art and Design Studies will be appropriate for this part of the question. In a full answer, candidates should deal with aspects of portraiture such as likeness, personality mood, expression and communication from a personal viewpoint.

   Differences in the artists' treatment of these aspects should be made evident. Comparisons and contrasts in approaches may include: use of visual elements, styles and ways in which your selected artists use materials and media.

2. **Figure Composition**
   (*a*) In this part of the question, candidates can provide a wide range of valid personal responses about the appeal of this work. Responses that deal specifically with the contribution of each selected visual element will gain high marks.

   The use of shape may provoke references to the variety of playful poses and the patterns of clothing. The contrast in shape of the different compositional elements should be noted in a very good answer.

   Linear qualities are evident throughout the work and candidates should recognise this in clothing/use of the steps and wall to create perspective space/contrast in line between fine and thick.

   Candidates can link colour and tone to the strong directional light from the left and the darker spaces in the background/tunnel.

   (*b*) Candiates should demonstrate knowledge and understanding of two figure compositions studied in their work for Art and Design Studies. Candidates should give personal opinions of the artists' work and reasoned judgements on their success or otherwise.

   Candidates who can demonstrate understanding of their selected artists' approaches by considering choice of media, styles, subject matter, compositional and visual elements etc, will be very well rewarded.

   Discussion should be supported by reasoned opinion about each aspect or approach identified.

3. **Still Life**
   (*a*) Candiates could comment on the use of more than three visual elements in this work and will be credited for appropriate identification of their relevance to the work, however brief.

The use of 'real' texture in the oysters should be noted. Some speculation on Caulfield's intention in making one part of the picture real and the rest flat, illustrative, and decorative should be responded to. Comment on the oysters being shown both in outline and in highly realistic detail will be made in a good answer.

Brief comment should be made on the use of bold flat colour and the comparison of this unusual approach to more traditional media methods of still life could also be made.

The work may be linked to Pop Art. The bold and lush colourful work of Patrick Caulfield can be termed 'pop art' because of his use of unusual flat shapes and the contemporary setting. Identification of the work as an interior, possibly a kitchen, with light coming from an open window, basket of leeks sitting on the table, painted with thick black outlines should be made. The contrast created by the oysters shown both in outline and in highly realistic detail should allow speculation on the artist's intentions.

Consideration of line in terms of the thick outlines of the objects making them stand out as if they can be touched will be credited.

Descriptions of the work as decorative, illustrative, flat, or graphic will be rewarded.

Candidates may refer to composition as in the very random arrangement of the objects when giving your opinion on the work.

(b) In this very open-ended part of the question candidates can draw from a wide ranging study of still-life. In a good response to this part of the question there should be evidence that still-lifes have been selected which are contrasting in terms of composition, styles, working methods, materials, media used, and differing qualities such as abstract/ realistic, flat/solid. The still-life theme is very open and can include a wide range of traditional historical approaches as well as diverse contemporary interpretations of the theme. Well-justified personal opinions and analysis of particular examples will be expected in a very good answer.

4. **Natural Environment**

(a) Candidates should comment on the contribution of each of the identified aspects of the work. These might include the loose, impressionistic style and broad energetic handling of the medium, the expression of light and colour in clouds and sea and the rapid rough brushwork and naturalistic colour.

Candidates who link McTaggart's skilful handling of media and the visual elements with the successful depiction of the violent forces of nature and point to the passing effects of light on water/lashing wind/heaving water and crashing waves will be well rewarded.

Candidates may speculate, appropriately, that the work was painted out of doors. Candidates who also identify McTaggart's subject as the fragility of man and his struggle against the elements and violent forces of nature will be very well rewarded.

(b) This part of the question is open to a variety of personal responses including straightforward compare and contrast of familiar landscape artists such as Turner and Constable to more site-specific contemporary work. Valid comparison based on knowledge of the individual approaches of the selected artists should be apparent in the answer.

Styles, working methods, materials, media handling, use of visual elements and 2D/3D approaches represent the range of possible comment which could form the basis of a well-constructed response.

All analysis should be backed up by well-substantiated personal opinions.

5. **Built Environment**

(a) Candidates should have an awareness of how Utrillo uses some visual elements in this work. Since almost all visual elements are present in the work, candidates must select the most important, in their opinion.

Comment will be expected on line to create depth and perspective and contrast through the horizontal line of the shutters and the verticals of the trees.

Colour should be identified in the bright shop fronts and cafes along with the thick paintwork to create contrast.

Shape should be understood in the structure of the buildings windows, doors and the variety and balance throughout the work.

Texture is evident in the handling of the brushwork and application of paint.

When commenting on the successful depiction of the quiet atmosphere of the work, candidates may offer judgements about the time of day. Overall, it may be considered that the work is a little postcard-like or too nice and picturesque but credit will be given for well-justified negative views.

(b) This part of the question allows candidates to consider a wide range of work in this theme. It requires the demonstration of knowledge and understanding of the different approaches used by the chosen artists and a reasoned opinion to be given on the success of the works. This may well lead candidates to select from a wide range of artists within the given range. A good answer will include some understanding of the artists' treatment of particular aspects of the built environment from a personal viewpoint. Since the theme of built environment is broad, a range of historically important artists may be selected as well as contemporary artists. It would be possible to compare artists who paint the built environment with artists such as Mach, Hirst, and Whiteread who create built environment using a range of approaches. Your discussion should cover explanations of similarities and differences in the selected works as well as personal comment/preferences on the use of media by both artists.

6. **Fantasy and Imagination**

(a) Candidates should be able to establish the sense of threat and fear through the imposing compositional arrangement in this work.

Consideration should be given to the artist's vision of the dragon done in hues of ochre and reddish brown, seen from behind to emphasise his great tail. This would represent a very good analysis of colour when compared to the lighter hues used to focus on the woman and should be present in a very good response.

In addition, comments on the composition should recognise the dominant position of the figure of Satan.

A very good response will connect the dragon with a representation of Satan/Devil.

Any comment on the power and threat in the pose with outspread legs and the fragility of the women will be credited very highly.

Credit will be given to the linking of the effects of light to the contrast of good and evil.

Comment on the huge extended wings over the woman clothed with the sun, who is depicted in gold with a pale yellow moon at her feet, and the sense of threat and fear would mark out a very good response.

Attempts to associate Blake's visionary/dream experiences as symbols of the battle between good and evil will be well rewarded.

Identification of elements of fantasy such as exaggeration, distortion and changes of scale will be well rewarded.

(b) This part of the question should encourage candidates who have studied fantasy and imagination through surrealist art, to select obvious works such as those of Dali, Magritte and Di Chirico. Compare and contrast should include comparison of identified elements of fantasy and imagination in the selected works. Well-justified opinions to substantiate preferences will be present in very good answers to this part of the question.

Design Studies

7. Graphic Design

(a) Opinions concerning imagery should refer to the depiction of the characters on the front cover. Comment should be made on how the use of the shadowy, hooded main character adds a sense of mystery. Reference should be made to clothing and pose, as well as the background effect. Candidates could speculate on reasons for the older character in the background being depicted in tones of blue. Good answers should refer to the stylisation of the images and how the designer has made the characters look powerful.

In discussing layout, candidates may comment on how the designer has communicated different aspects of the game through the row of character portraits on the back cover and the screenshots. Comment may be made about the screenshots, which capture stills of fight scenes in the game. It may be concluded that these effectively show the type of action to be expected and some of the different settings.

The positioning and scale of the lettering may be discussed. Reference could be made to the lettering style of the game's title. Candidates could comment on the blurb on the back and the use of bold text to highlight certain information.

Candidates should give opinions about how well the cover has been designed for its purpose, and relevant, well justified comments will be credited.

(b) Answers should demonstrate knowledge and understanding of the work of two different graphic designers. Reference should be made to the selected examples of work to enable comment on how the designers achieved visual impact and originality. Candidates should demonstrate knowledge of appropriate terminology concerning relevant design issues. Answers may focus on two design movements or styles of graphic design.

8. Product Design

(a) In terms of style, candidates may comment on the geometric semi-spherical appearance of the teapot and its circular off-centre lid. Candidates may demonstrate knowledge of Art Deco style or note its simplicity and modern appearance for its time.

When discussing function, practical issues such as balance and stability may be addressed. Opinion may be given on the effectiveness of the unusual solution to the 'feet' of the teapot. Candidates may also speculate on how easy it might be to fill and pour the teapot, perhaps commenting on the solid handle.

In describing the use of materials, it may be noted that silver is a relatively expensive material for a teapot and it may be concluded that the product may not be intended for everyday use. Heat conducting properties of the materials may be discussed, with reference to the fact that the wooden handle would prevent the user from being burnt when picking up the teapot.

Substantiated opinions, positive or negative, on how well the designer has combined these issues will be rewarded.

(b) This question requires a demonstration of knowledge and understanding of the work of two different designers. The nature of the question calls for focus on two design issues from a choice of style, use of materials, function and methods of construction. Good answers should contain comparative comment and show an understanding of appropriate design terminology. Answers may focus on two design movements or styles.

9. Interior Design

(a) Candidates should give substantiated opinions on the suitability of this interior as an upmarket restaurant. In reference to use of space, candidates may comment on the use of booths, creating a more intimate atmosphere. The amount of space around the tables may be discussed, and it may be noticed that this is quite generous, allowing plenty of room for waiting staff and more privacy for diners. When commenting on furniture and fittings, candidates may write about the specially built-in furniture and the way curves are used throughout the restaurant. The plush materials chosen for the upholstery could be discussed. The advantages of the choice of round tables may be debated, and the coordinating round-backed chairs could elicit opinions. Choice of light fittings may provoke a response. The co-ordinated colour scheme of warm pinks and ambers, accented by green, and the atmosphere created, may be discussed. Attention to detail could be noted.

Candidates may speculate on how well they think the space fulfils its function as an upmarket restaurant. Relevant, well justified points will be awarded marks.

(b) This question requires a demonstration of knowledge and understanding of the work of two interior designers. Answers should refer to two specific interiors focusing on two design issues from a choice of style, use of space, use of lighting and use of materials. Good answers should demonstrate a sound understanding of design terminology. Answers may focus on two design movements or styles.

10. Environmental/Architectural Design

(a) This question requires candidates to make a judgement on the success of this design in relation to certain design issues. Good answers should justify opinion specifically in terms of form, function and scale.

Candidates may describe the sculptural form of the structure, noting that its form is largely dictated by its function.

When commenting on function, candidates should be able to deduce from the images and legend, the purpose of the wheel and the basic principles of how it operates. Comment may be made on the feat of engineering involved in linking the two waterways. Candidates should make reference to the vast scale of the structure, and how it dominates the surrounding landscape.

(b) This question requires a demonstration of knowledge and understanding of the work of two environmental/ architectural designers. With reference to two specific works, candidates should comment on fitness for purpose and style. Good answers will use appropriate design terminology and make well justified points. Answers may be based on two design movements or styles.

11. Jewellery Design

(a) Candidates should realise that the main function of this type of jewellery is to show wealth and status in society. It may also be understood that this sort of antique jewellery may be passed down through the generations, and is often sought after by collectors. Candidates may comment on the fact that this jewellery would only be worn on certain occasions, being too impractical and heavy, (not to mention expensive), to wear on a regular basis.

When discussing style, candidates may comment on the large scale of the jewellery, particularly the brooch. The (neo) classical form may be recognised and the regular, symmetrical nature of the pattern may be noted. Sources of inspiration might be guessed at, concluding that natural forms have been the original influence, based on the stylised leaf-like forms.

Comment should be made about the expensive nature of the materials, which contributes to the precious, rare quality of the pieces. Comments could also be made about the skill required to work with such materials.

In terms of target market, candidates should conclude that these jewellery pieces would have been specially commissioned for one individual at the time they were made, and that owners of this jewellery would be very wealthy. Candidates may discuss the fact that the jewellery has been designed for a female.

(b) This part of the question requires a knowledge and understanding of the work of two jewellery designers. Two specific examples should be discussed. Comment should be made on the designers' style and use of materials. Good answers should include comparative analysis. Answers may focus on two design movements or styles.

12. Textile/Fashion Design

(a) This question allows candidates to make comments on this outfit based on their knowledge and understanding of textile/fashion design issues and their own observations of formal menswear. Good answers should discuss differences between this historical outfit and contemporary formal menswear with specific reference to style, function, and wearability.

Candidates may conclude that the style of the historical outfit is more flamboyant than typical examples of modern men's formal wear. Descriptive terminology may refer to the high-waist knee-length trousers, the ruffled cuffs and shirt collar, the double-breasted cut-away jacket, the long coat tails, and wide lapels.

Attention to detail, such as the pockets, and large buttons, and their positioning, should be noted. The accessories, with their co-ordinating large buckles, and their overall effect on the outfit should be commented on. The choice of the striped yellow fabric for the jacket may be regarded as unconventional.

In commenting on function, candidates may give opinions about the purpose of formal menswear generally.

It may be noted that this is a special occasion outfit, and that it may enhance the person's standing in society, showing off their wealth and status. It may be noted that the outfit is designed to help the wearer stand out in the crowd.

In discussing wearability, candidates may speculate on how comfortable the outfit might be compared with contemporary examples. Perceived inconveniences, such as the length of the coat tails, the number of buttons and the long length of the sleeves could be discussed.

(b) Candidates should compare the work of two textile/fashion designers with reference to two specific examples of their work. Good answers should include comparative comments and demonstrate knowledge and understanding of style and target market. Answers may focus on two design movements or styles.

ART AND DESIGN INTERMEDIATE 2 2009

OVERVIEW

The Art and Design Studies Examination Component 2 – Question Paper has been set with the following principles in mind:

1. The examination set for Art and Design Studies at Intermediate 2 level should clearly articulate with the Higher level. The format of the Intermediate 2 examination paper is therefore similar to the Higher paper with respect to the reference materials used and the six headed questions in each of the two sections: Art Studies and Design Studies.

2. Intermediate 2 candidates are required to demonstrate knowledge and understanding of selected aspects of the visual arts and design and to formulate, explain and communicate personal opinions and conclusions. The format of the questions reflects this emphasis. Each question has two equally demanding parts.

   Parts (a) and (b) are designed to test the candidates' ability to respond critically to a range of visual arts imagery and design products and to form and substantiate judgements about identified aspects of art practice and design issues. The questions also require candidates to demonstrate knowledge and understanding gained through their Art and Design Studies as follows:

Part (a)

This part of the question requires candidates to give an analytical response to a selected illustration from the supplied reference materials using appropriate terminology and making reference to identified aspects of Art and Design practice.

Part (b)

This part of the question requires candidates to make a personal critical response to identified visual elements and art practice in Section 1 of the paper and to identify visual aspects and design issues in Section 2 of the paper. Candidates are expected to substantiate reasons to support judgements and personal opinions expressed in their responses to this part of the question.

3. All questions are of equal demand. The questions should be suitable for candidates with a relatively detailed knowledge as well as those whose knowledge is more wide ranging.

4. It is important that candidates respond with answers, to this part of the question, that contain a depth of knowledge and understanding of their specialist area of the visual arts and design. In these instances, candidates should be well rewarded.

   Candidates are expected to demonstrate their knowledge and understanding with reference to specific artworks/designs. Responses which contain only historical and/or biographical information and which do not fully address the question can gain a maximum of only **5 marks**.

   At this level, candidates are rewarded for naming their selected artists and designers and the corresponding artworks and designs which they intend to discuss in their answers. A maximum of **1 mark** is available within each part (b) response for this information.

   Candidates who discuss only one artist/designer in a part (b) response cannot have fully answered the question set. In this case, a maximum of **7 marks** can be awarded.

5. In Art Studies questions, where the term "artist" is used it should be interpreted in its broadest sense, covering painting, printmaking, photography, sculpture, installation, animation, film and video.

6. Similarly in the Design Studies questions, the term "designer" should be inclusive of any form of design.

Art Studies

1. Portraiture – Stephen Conroy, Self Portrait

(a) In response to this part of the question, candidates should be given credit for well-justified personal opinions about the impact of the artist's use of *tone, shape* and composition in the work.

The question asks candidates to link the use of these elements to the expression of emotion. Some candidates may identify the emotion with the fact that it is a self portrait and offer comment on how the artist might have been feeling at the time. Very good responses will interpret the downward gaze of the artist in the selected pose in the **composition** as signifying unhappiness, shyness, introspection, even self absorption and intensity.

Expect Good candidates will recognise that Conroy uses strong **tone** and modelling in the head to give solidity and realism to the work. Some may conclude that this adds a troubled look to the portrait.

Conroy has deliberately created a ghosted halo form around the figure against a very boldly stated cross. Some candidates may link this to the emotional impact of the work and should be well rewarded.

The strong contrast between geometric **shape** and the figure may seem to contribute to the impact of the work. Any well-justified comment should be credited.

(b) Any significant portraiture within the range period set for Art and Design Studies will be appropriate for this part of the question. A full answer should show that the candidate has appropriate knowledge and understanding of two different artists. The question calls for the candidate to give opinions which are well justified. To do this, clear reference should be made to aspects such as the styles, approaches and intentions of the artists as well as visual elements, media handling and composition.

2. Figure Composition – Douane Hanson, Tourists

(a) This part of the question will provoke a wide range of opinions about the impact of this work. The wording of the question allows candidates to consider the work from three standpoints.

Some candidates may speculate that Hanson chose the **subject** because he wanted to show ordinary life in very unusual ways and should be credited. Equally, they may identify mockery, caricature as the reason for the choice of subject.

Those candidates who see the **pose** as catching the figures off guard, frozen in a moment of time or as successful because the artist has captured them in the act of being typical tourists should be well rewarded.

It is expected that almost all candidates will in some way link the choice of **media** to Hanson's hyper realistic approach, they may suggest that the figures remind them of tailors' dummies posed to suggest a particular way of life and comment on the use of real articles of clothing either positively or negatively. In each case this would be a valid response.

(b) Candidates should demonstrate knowledge and understanding of two figure compositions studied in their work for Art and Design Studies. They should give personal opinions of the artists' work and reasoned judgements on their success or otherwise.

Those candidates who can demonstrate understanding of their selected artists' approaches by considering choice of media, styles, subject matter, compositional and visual elements, etc should be very well rewarded. Discussion should be supported by reasoned opinion about each aspect or approach identified by the candidate.

3. Still Life – Richard Diebenkorn, Still Life

(a) This part of the question asks the candidate to give opinion on what may be considered an unusual still life by some.

The absence of colour means that the candidate has to offer comment on the use of the monochrome **media** in the work. Any well-justified comments, positive of negative should be rewarded here. Balance between light and dark areas would be an obvious point recognised by many candidates. Recognition of the sketchy, unfinished or even spontaneous approach may be appreciated by some candidates as contributing to the impact of the work.

As still life is a popular practical theme, candidates should be familiar with some of the formal elements of **composition** and thus be able to give an opinion of almost random arrangement and viewpoint chosen by Diebenkorn. They may find the choice of **subject matter** unattractive and point to the absence of any formal compositional arrangement. They might also reflect that the objects are not the most appropriate for still life. In either case, these comments, well justified, should be given credit.

(b) In response to this part of the question, candidates may select from a wide range of approaches to still life studied for the course.

In a good response to this part of the question there will be evidence that the candidate has selected still lifes which are contrasting in terms of the handling of media.

This would include contrasting, eg an Impressionist still life with a Cubist approach.

Comment on the use of visual elements is expected. This may be strong use of colour and shape in, for example, a Matisse still life with the smoother realism of 19th century examples.

Well-justified opinions backed up with reasons are expected in a very good answer to this part of the question.

4. Natural Environment – Horatio McCulloch

(a) All candidates should comment on the contribution of each of the identified aspects of the work to gain maximum marks.

A very good response will relate the artist's use of the visual elements to the mood and atmosphere of the painting. **Tone** may be seen to contribute to the solidity and depth of the exposed landscape and the creation of wide desolate lonely places. Some candidates might link tone to the artist's use of arial perspective and should be very well rewarded. Comments on the **composition** of the landscape scene which suggest scale, grandeur and the awe inspiring sight of the mountains would also gain marks, as would comments on the use of strong shadow created by the partially clouded sky.

Some candidates may conjecture on the presence of the deer and the track road in the distance and may link this to the mood of the painting.

Straightforward links between the artist's use of earth naturalistic **colour** and the wild rugged landscape along with the effects of weather should also gain marks for candidates.

(b) In this part of the question, candidates should demonstrate their knowledge and understanding of, for example, methods, approaches styles, influences and use of visual elements of their selected artists. The selected artists may come from a range of historical and contemporary periods or styles.

5. Built Environment

(a) This part of the question requires the candidate to comment on Derain's use of visual elements and his handling of media.

A very good response is likely to contain comment on the vibrant, bold and expressive use of **colour**. Some candidates may comment on the unnatural effect of the colour, pointing to the use of yellows and greens to represent the strong ripples on the water, the blues of the background buildings and the pink sky to support their view and conclude that it represents a particular time of day.

A good response will also offer comment on the use of the **medium** as spontaneous, energetic, loose or even jagged, rough and unfinished looking to describe Derain's approach. Candidates who recognise the way in which Derain has used broken brushstrokes to describe the activity of the traffic on the bridge and the movement of the barge as contributing to the busy scene should be well rewarded.

To complete a very good response, the candidate should recognise Derain's bold simplified use of **shape** in the buildings, the bridge and the bridge traffic, perhaps offering comment on the effectiveness of this approach.

(b) For this part of the question, candidates may select from a wide range of artists and artworks associated with the theme of built environment. The question requires the candidate to demonstrate their knowledge and understanding of the different media and methods used by their chosen artists.

This may include very diverse approaches including artists who construct environments in the form of installation or tableaux, along with artists whose principal aim is to respond, using traditional media to cityscape such as Hopper and Pissarro.

Clear explanation of the differences in media and understanding of the methods used by the artist are required in a very good answer. Well-reasoned opinions on the success of the works are required. This may well lead good candidates to select from a wide range of art works within the given range. A good answer will include some understanding of the artists' treatment of particular aspects of the built environment from a personal viewpoint. Since the theme of built environment is broad, a range of historically important artists may be selected as well as contemporary artists.

Candidates may well compare artists who paint the built environment with artists such as Mach, Hirst and Whiteread who create built environment using a range of approaches.

The discussion should cover explanations of similarities and differences in the selected works as well as personal comment/preferences on the use of media by both artists.

6. Fantasy and imagination

(a) This part of the question is set to give candidates scope to respond in several ways. Candidates who recognise some of the familiar devices used by surrealist artists in their work should score well. These would be unusual juxtapositions, changes in scale and strange impossible dreamlike imagery.

Some may relate the imagery to the sea and recognise that Wadsworth has used objects that would be found on the beach in new and strange relationships.

Expect comments on the use of visual elements to include some consideration of the use of colour to add to the improbable world created by Wadsworth or the contrast between the sunny beach and the strange scene unfolding on it.

Some candidates may be able to recognise strong linear qualities linking the various parts of the composition and should be well rewarded for this observation.

(b) Candidates' discussion should demonstrate knowledge and understanding of the particular approaches of artists who are recognised as working within this theme. Those who clearly identify the different approaches and sources used by artists associated with, eg Symbolism, Surrealism and Romanticism should be able to refer to identified methods and approaches belonging to these styles and should be able to score highly.

Some knowledge of the identified style of the artist, particularly surrealism with its clear associations with the theme will be expected and given credit.

Candidates who offer preferences based on well-justified reasons should be credited.

7. Graphic Design

(a) Candidates should speculate on the likely target market. Many will come to the conclusion that the design is aimed at both children and their parents. In justifying their opinions, reference should be made to imagery, lettering and colour.

In discussing imagery, the stylised cartoon bird character should elicit comment as should the depiction of the breakfast cereal. The style and placement of the lettering should be discussed. The selection of bright colours combined with brown (with its connotations of chocolate) should be discussed in terms of its success and likely attraction for the target market. Candidates may comment on the inclusion of nutritional information and the use of the standard 'traffic light' colour scheme. The choice of green to convey some aspects of nutritional information may also provoke comment.

Candidates should give opinions generally about the success of this design. Opinions may be positive or negative. Well-justified comments should be credited.

(b) Answers should demonstrate knowledge and understanding of the work of two different graphic designers. Reference should be made to the selected examples of work to enable the candidate to comment on how the designers have created effective designs with visual impact. Methods used should be identified and discussed. Candidates should demonstrate knowledge of appropriate graphic design terminology and relevant design issues. It is acceptable for answers to focus on two design movements or styles of graphic design.

8. Product Design

(a) This question gives ample scope for candidates to compare this gramophone to contemporary products.

Comparison should address the design issues of appearance and function. However, it is not necessary for candidates to demonstrate a knowledge of how the product actually works in that the sound is generated through a needle moving across the grooves of a record, as this technology will be unfamiliar to many candidates.

Candidates may discuss the gramophone's winding mechanism and compare this with how present day music systems are powered. Advantages and disadvantages of this system may be noted. Most candidates should realise that the sound is emitted from the horn, which operates like a speaker. The size of the product may generate comment, particularly when compared to today's much smaller and more technologically advanced systems. The limited functions may be discussed in comparison to the wide range of contemporary multi-functional products capable of playing music.

The appearance of the product can be compared to today's less decorative music players. The shape of the horn may be compared with natural forms, such as a flower opening out. The carving on the wooden base may be noted. The function of the product as a piece of furniture, or in fitting in with interior décor, may be discussed. Candidates may discuss the contrast of the shiny metallic horn and the wooden base.

Well-justified comparative comments showing an understanding of appropriate design terminology should be rewarded.

(b) This question requires the candidate to demonstrate a knowledge and understanding of the work of two different product designers. Reference should be made to one product by each designer. Answers should focus on how the designers have created these products to be functional and visually appealing. Therefore, candidates are required to show an understanding of functional and aesthetic issues in product design.

Depending on the choice of designers, it is possible that a candidate may conclude that a particular product is not functional and/or visually appealing. If this conclusion is backed up with well reasoned opinion, then credit should be given. It is perfectly acceptable for answers to focus on two design movements or styles.

9. Interior Design

(a) Candidates are required to state their opinion on how well the designers have created a stylish interior. In doing so, they should make reference to structure, use of space and materials.

In discussing structure, candidates should comment on the curved form of the ceiling and the repetition of the structural elements. There may be speculation on likely sources of inspiration. The use of colour in emphasising the structure may also elicit comment.

Candidates may discuss the way the space is divided up within the spacious interior. Good answers should refer to the double height spaces and use of mezzanine levels. The use of signposting to guide the users through the terminal may be discussed.

Candidates may note the contrast of natural and man-made materials and discuss the qualities, properties and suitability of these materials. It may be noted that the use or glass, to allow natural light in, contributes to the airy atmosphere.

Whether or not the designers have achieved a stylish interior may generate a positive or negative response. Relevant, well-justified points should be awarded marks.

(b) This question requires a demonstration of knowledge and understanding of the work of two interior designers. Answers should refer to two specific interiors. Key design issues should be identified which contribute to the interiors' success aesthetically and in meeting the needs of the users. Good answers will contain some comparative comment.

Well-justified opinion should be rewarded. It is acceptable for answers to concentrate on two design movements or styles.

10. Environmental/Architectural Design

(a) This question requires candidates to show an understanding of how form, decoration and scale contribute to this building's sense of importance.

Good answers will comment on the classically inspired form of this historic building, with its symmetry created by the placement of the structural pillars and application of decoration to the stonework. The imposing form of the domed roof should be noted. The difficulty in constructing such a building and the need for specialist craftspeople in creating the form and decoration may be discussed, along with the time taken to complete the building.

In commenting on the decoration in more detail, candidates should discuss the repetition of certain motifs, the carved figures, the shape of the windows and the gold statues.

The scale of the building is made clear through comparison with the surrounding objects, particularly the cars parked in front, and candidates should be able to discuss the fact that this is a large and impressive building.

Most candidates will conclude that these elements do create a sense of grandeur and importance.

(b) This question requires a demonstration of knowledge and understanding of the work of two environmental/ architectural designers. Candidates should refer to two specific works, commenting specifically on style, materials and purpose. Good answers will use appropriate terminology and make well-reasoned points. It is acceptable for answers to be based on two design movements or styles of environmental/architectural design.

11. Jewellery Design

(a) This question requires candidates to give their opinion of this watch, commenting specifically on style, materials and fitness for purpose.

Although made in 1942, candidates may recognise the Art Deco styling of this watch. Even if this is not the case, they should be able to discuss the geometric form and the use of repeating elements.

When discussing materials, candidates should realise that expensive precious metals and stones have been used, which would mean that this is an upmarket product. There may be comment on the success of the choice of materials.

Functional issues should be addressed in discussing fitness for purpose. There may be comment on how easily the time could be read and how the watch may be fastened. The flexible strap may be noticed and comment made on how this would increase the comfort of the wearer. The function of the watch as a status symbol as well as a timepiece may elicit a response. There may be speculation on who might wear such a watch. Relevant, well-justified opinion should be rewarded.

(b) This part of the question requires a knowledge and understanding of the work of two jewellery designers. Two specific examples should be selected. The designers' sources of inspiration and techniques should be compared. Good answers will address the issue of whether visually exciting pieces of jewellery have been created. Well-justified opinions should be credited.

Answers may focus on two design movements or styles of jewellery design and this is perfectly acceptable.

12. Textile/Fashion Design

(a) This question requires candidates to give their opinion on the success of this outfit with particular reference to sources of inspiration, form and detail.

Candidates may speculate on sources of inspiration, although the 'Dinosaur' title will give them a clue as to the idea behind the zig-zag edging. Other sources of inspiration may be identified as flowers. Good answers will discuss the designer's interpretation of these sources and her use of simplified, stylised shapes.

The construction may be discussed when commenting on form. It may be noted that the seams are on the outside, with the raw edges showing. The use of felt means that the edges have not frayed, but have retained their shape. The use of thick felt has also contributed to the 3-dimensional, sculptural form of the coat. The unusual feature of the scalloped edge on the hemline may be discussed.

Candidates should notice the use of detail in the applied flower decoration and the co-ordinating flower-patterned lining used on the coat. The placing of the appliqué flowers may be discussed.

Positive or negative opinions may be expressed regarding the success of the outfit, as long as they are well reasoned and justified

(b) This question requires candidates to show a knowledge and understanding of the work of two textile/fashion designers. Two specific examples of their work should be discussed with reference to sources of inspiration and use of materials. Good answers will show an understanding of how the selected examples relate to each designer's individual style. It is acceptable for answers to focus on two design movements or styles.

ART AND DESIGN INTERMEDIATE 2 2010

OVERVIEW

The Art and Design Studies Examination Component 2 – Question Paper has been set with the following principles in mind:

1. The examination set for Art and Design Studies at Intermediate 2 level should clearly articulate with the Higher level. The format of the Intermediate 2 examination paper is therefore similar to the Higher paper with respect to the reference materials used and the six headed questions in each of the two sections: Art Studies and Design Studies.

2. Intermediate 2 candidates are required to demonstrate knowledge and understanding of selected aspects of the visual arts and design and to formulate, explain and communicate personal opinions and conclusions. The format of the questions reflects this emphasis. Each question has two equally demanding parts.

Parts (a) and (b) are designed to test the candidates' ability to respond critically to a range of visual arts imagery and design products and to form and substantiate judgements about identified aspects of art practice and design issues. The questions also require candidates to demonstrate knowledge and understanding gained through their Art and Design Studies as follows:

Part (a)
This part of the question requires candidates to give an analytical response to a selected illustration from the supplied reference materials using appropriate terminology and making reference to identified aspects of Art and Design practice. The questions set require candidates to discuss specific art/design issues. While judgement and flexibility should be applied by the marker, candidates who do not address all aspects of the question cannot be awarded full marks.

Part (b)
This part of the question requires candidates to make a personal critical response to identified visual elements and art practice in Section 1 of the paper and to identify visual aspects and design issues in Section 2 of the paper. Candidates are expected to substantiate reasons to support judgements and personal opinions expressed in their responses to this part of the question.

3. All questions are of equal demand. The questions should be suitable for candidates with a relatively detailed knowledge as well as those whose knowledge is more wide ranging.

4. Overall, the examination paper makes certain demands on markers, particularly with regard to part (b) of each question. It is possible that candidates will have studied artists and designers of whom little is known to the marker. In such cases, the marker would have to use his or her professional experience and consider how likely it is that an apparently detailed, informative and thoughtful answer is the spontaneous invention of some ill-informed candidate.

The overriding advice to markers would be to consider if the answer is evidence of any specialist knowledge and understanding of an identifiable area of the visual arts or design. If a candidate who had not followed an Art or Design course or unit of Art and Design Studies and demonstrated no specialist knowledge and understanding could have written the answer, then very little credit could be given.

It is important to consider, however, that candidates can and will respond with answers, to this part of the question, that contain a depth of knowledge and understanding of their specialist area of the visual arts and design. In these instances, candidates should be well rewarded.

Candidates are expected to demonstrate their knowledge and understanding with reference to specific artworks/designs. Responses which contain only historical and/or biographical information and which do not fully address the question can gain a maximum of only **5 marks**.

At this level, candidates are rewarded for naming their selected artists and designers and the corresponding artworks and designs which they intend to discuss in their answers. A maximum of **1 mark** is available within each part (b) response for this information.

Candidates who discuss only one artist/designer in a part (b) response cannot have fully answered the question set. In this case, a maximum of **7 marks** can be awarded.

5. In Art Studies questions, where the term "artist" is used it should be interpreted in its broadest sense, covering painting, printmaking, photography, sculpture, installation, animation, film and video.

6. Similarly in the Design Studies questions, the term "designer" should be inclusive of any form of design.

Art Studies

1. Portraiture

(a) This question should allow the candidate to describe and give justified reason for this artist's use of *pose, tone* and *colour* in this work.

Pose: The candidate may make reference to the dramatic pose, the sitter looking directly at the viewer and may offer an interpretation of this in light of the title of this work.

Tone: Comments on the use of tone to create drama and the effects of lighting may be offered by the candidate.

Colour: The candidate may make comments on the limited use of colour and may offer reasons why this is. All of the above may form part of candidates' responses and should be fully rewarded.

A full answer will include comments which cover the relationship the artist attempts to make with the viewer.

(b) Candidates answering this question should use two examples of portraiture by two artists who they can show a knowledge and understanding of. A very sound response must deal with visual elements used in their work. Comment may be made on mood, expression and pose. Candidates may speculate on working methods and media used.

The candidates should be able to discuss the ways in which the artists' have selected and used materials and media. They may also wish to comment on the social aspects of the times that the works were produced in.

- Well linked to movements by using knowledge and understanding.

- Able to discuss aspects of visual elements line, where tone and also the impact they have on us the viewer. Bold, fascinating, adding detail, restricted not varied portrayed gloomy and dark atmosphere line to help image stand out.

2. Figure Composition

(a) This part of the question should provoke a range of valid personal responses about the situation portrayed in this work. Comparisons with their own everyday circumstances may be given and if relevant to the work should be rewarded. The title may well be discussed in light of the candidates own knowledge of video games and this should again be well rewarded.

A good answer will have the candidate make valid comment with justification on the use of *colour, light* and *composition.*

Colour: Comments on the use of colour to create this realistic work may be offered and where justified should be well rewarded.

Light: The candidate may offer their interpretation as to the use of light, natural or artificial in this work and may make reference to areas in the work to justify this.

Composition: Comments that offer an interpretation of the setting and the characters in this work where justified should be well rewarded.

(b) Candidates should attempt to discuss the works of two artists who have worked within the genre of figure composition. A very good response should be the selection of two pieces that typify the artists' response to figure composition. They may wish to discuss artists whose work reflects the historical or indeed the contemporary works that can be viewed as figurative today.

3. Still Life

(a) In this question the candidate will be expected to justify opinions made on this artist's choice of *subject matter.* They may then give as broad or as selective a set of comments that cover the visual elements that they see at work in this painting. Marks should be awarded to those that are justified in some manner. Here candidates may refer to the visual elements they see as the strongest in the work, the portrayal of surfaces and textures or the use of colour and tone to suggest realism in forms in the work.

The simple arrangement and the slick handling of technique may also be mentioned and these should be well rewarded.

(b) The candidates should show their knowledge and understanding of still-life through the discussion and analysis of two artists and two typical works. A very good response will be one that is structured, to show that there is a comparison and contrast of the works selected, with regards to differing styles and techniques. The still-life genre is very open and you can expect a wide range of approaches studies from the historical to the contemporary.

4. Natural Environment

(a) Markers should expect and credit the candidates initial feelings on how well this frosty morning scene has been painted. Remarks about the possible working methods and selection of the composition, if made, should be well rewarded.

For a full answer the candidate should have referred to and justified the use of all three of the key elements asked for, these being *colour, mood* and *technique.*

Colour: Candidates should be fully rewarded for any links that they make between the artists use of muted colour to suggest the feeling of a frosty morning. Candidates may also offer comments on areas of colour within the work to justify their responses.

Mood: Here candidates may offer a range of individual ideas on how the mood is captured for the viewer, they may well make reference to the foreground and background, the lack of people populating the scene or the rural location. When justified these should be fully rewarded.

Technique: Candidates may attempt to justify the handling of the material by the artist and refer to individual areas of the work in justifying this to discuss where the technique is best seen in action, these points should be fully rewarded.

(b) This part of the question is open to a variety of personal responses that include examples taken from a wide range of interpretations. To the theme of the natural environment. To gain full marks the candidate should have made some attempt to discuss, with justifications, points made on individual responses to the natural environment. The candidates should display a knowledge and understanding of Art Terminology in relation to the theme.

5. Built Environment

(a) In this question the candidate will share their opinions on this relief work and in doing so should treat it as such, to gain the maximum award of ten marks.

Candidates would be expected to respond to this work through the information given in the legend.

For *scale, composition* and *texture*, a good answer should deal with each of these elements in light of the size, viewpoint and surface qualities that are on display to the viewer.

This work, for some candidates may elicit negative responses, these should be rewarded where they are justified.

(b) Candidates should demonstrate knowledge and understanding of two artists who use the built environment. They should give personal opinions of the artists' works that they have selected to discuss. Any points where the subject is discussed in a fashion that compares and contrasts should assist in gaining full marks.

Those candidates who demonstrate an understanding of the selected artists' methods and/or approaches should be well rewarded.

6. Fantasy and imagination

(a) This question will ask the candidate to firstly give opinions of the work; be aware of need to reward fully justified negative and positive points from candidates. At all times it should be noted that the candidates should be discussing the work with reference to it as a photograph to pick up full marks.

The candidates should be expected for full marks to include comments that relate to this work's *colour, scale* and *composition*.

Candidates may offer some justified explanation as to the grid that forms part of the work; valid well-made points should be fully rewarded.

Colour: The candidate may refer to primary and secondary colouring, the hand coloured legend information but should expand upon perhaps some interpretation of the technique employed to gain full marks on this point. Contrasting, bold in your face, colours blending in.

Scale: The candidate may reflect upon the size and relate this to viewing the work and how it may feel to the viewer.

Composition: The ideas and feelings that candidates may reflect upon may include the subject of life, god or religion and both human and botanical growth – Artists descending wings on suited figures.

Please note that the nature of this work may be commented upon more fully by candidates who understand the symbolic nature of these artists' thoughts and feelings or indeed may have studied them. If points are made with justification then marks may be awarded. Feelings of powerful work and incredible for viewer.

(b) This part of the question will allow candidates the display their knowledge of two artists whose work they know, who work within the theme of fantasy and imagination. You should expect well substantiated opinions of the typical works that they will compare and contrast for full marks.

The candidates may wish to cover the areas of working methods, media used, the artist's view of the world through fantasy and imaginative approaches. The work may span from the earliest examples to our most up to date contemporary artworks in this genre.

7. Graphic Design

(a) Candidates should give a response based on what they feel this poster communicates about the film. They should refer specifically to use of *lettering, colour* and *imagery*. In order to give a full answer, candidates should address all of these issues using appropriate terminology.

Lettering: Candidates may comment on the lettering style, scale, placement and what they feel the effect communicates about the film.

Colour: The designer's selection of colours and their effect should be discussed in terms of what is communicated about the film.

Imagery: The imagery used should give plenty of scope for discussion. Even if candidates do not understand the significance of the film title, they should still be able to comment on the feelings of confusion/suspense/danger/mystery generated.

The poster may provoke different opinions regarding what it says about the film and any reasonable, well justified comments should be rewarded.

(b) This question requires candidates to demonstrate knowledge and understanding of graphic design issues. **Two** specific examples of work by different designers should be selected. This will allow the candidates to compare the techniques used by the designers to create memorable graphic designs. Candidates should demonstrate knowledge of appropriate design terminology and relevant design issues.

8. Product Design

(a) This question asks candidates to give their opinions on why this product, designed in 1958, is still being sold successfully. Candidates may well have used the product themselves and may relate their comments to their own personal experience. To give a full response, candidates should refer specifically to *fitness for purpose, use of materials* and *target market*.

Fitness for purpose: Candidates should comment on the product's fitness for purpose and relate this to its ongoing success today.

Use of materials: The use of materials should be discussed and candidates are informed that the product is made from plastic. Candidates may relate the use of plastic to functional issues, such as durability, and aesthetic issues, such as style and appearance. Good answers will relate use of materials to the continuing success of the product.

Target market: Candidates should discuss the market(s) which they feel the toy appeals to. Good responses will be well justified and suggest reasons for the toy's enduring appeal to the target market.

Many candidates will be aware of how the toy has been developed and updated with different accessories. Although this knowledge is not a requirement, comments which relate this fact to why it is still successful today should be rewarded. Any relevant, well reasoned comment should be credited.

(b) This question requires a demonstration of knowledge and understanding of the work of **two** different product designers. Candidates are asked to discuss how the designers have created successful designs.

Candidates are directed to refer to **three** design issues from a choice of: *style; function; use of materials; sources of inspiration; use of technology*; and *target market*.

Candidates may conclude that certain designs are not entirely successful. As long as points made are well justified, marks should be awarded.

9. Interior Design

(a) Candidates are asked to compare this interior with more contemporary examples. They should be able to relate the historical interior to more up-to-date examples and there is abundant scope for discussion. There may be a variety of different opinions expressed depending on each candidate's own experience. Candidates are asked specifically to refer to *decoration; furnishings* and *use of space*.

Decoration: Opinions should be given on the decoration. Comments may be made about the colour scheme and choice of finishes, as well as the general ambience. In contrasting the décor of the historic interior with current examples, candidates should have ample opportunity for discussion.
Furnishings: Candidates should discuss the furnishings in relation to what you might expect to see in a cookery classroom today.
Use of space: The scale of the space may be discussed, as well as the way it is divided up. It is expected that candidates will comment on the raised platform at one end of the room, where the desks are arranged. The arrangement's suitability for the teaching of food preparation, in comparison with contemporary examples, should invite discussion.

Any valid, well reasoned points, whether positive or negative, should be rewarded.

(b) This question requires a demonstration of knowledge and understanding of the work of **two** interior designers. Answers should refer to specific interiors and explain the individual approaches used by the designers to create new and exciting interior spaces. It is acceptable for candidates to give positive or negative opinions on whether this has been achieved, so long as they are valid and well justified. Good answers will make effective use of design terminology and show an understanding of the key issues.

10. Environmental/Architectural Design

(a) Candidates are asked to give opinions on the success of this building in providing housing for a large number of families in an inner city environment. They are directed to refer to *form, function* and *scale* in their answers. Full answers will discuss all of these issues and use appropriate terminology.

Form: The stark, geometric form of the building should provoke comment. The arrangement of windows, balconies, bridges and walkways, as well as the separate tower, should provide subjects for discussion. Information is given on materials used, and candidates may use this in their response (eg the use of reinforced concrete to create the structural form).
Function: The function, to provide high density housing within a small area, should be discussed in relation to whether it is successful or not. Even candidates who do not have direct experience of this type of housing should be familiar with some of the issues through the media and through their general knowledge and understanding of architecture. Candidates may refer to social and environmental issues as well as practical considerations. Positive and negative features may be discussed.
Scale: The fact that the building is a high rise tower block should be discussed. Good answers will relate comments on the scale of the building to whether it is successful in providing housing for a number of families in the inner city.

Relevant well reasoned opinions as to the success of the building (or perceived lack of success) should be rewarded.

(b) This part of the question requires candidates to demonstrate their knowledge and understanding of the work of **two** environmental/architectural designers. Two designs should be selected for discussion. Full answers will comment effectively using appropriate terminology, on how *style, function* and *materials* have contributed to the success of each design.

11. Jewellery Design

(a) Candidates should discuss how *found materials* have been used to create this statement piece of jewellery. Candidates are also instructed to give their opinion on whether it is a successful design in terms of *style* and *wearability*.

Found materials: The choice and likely source of the materials could be discussed, along with comments on how they have been combined and put together.
Style: The style of the piece should provoke opinion. Candidates should attempt to describe the style and say whether they regard it as successful. The style of the piece may be liked or disliked and well justified points made in this respect should be rewarded. Good responses will relate the issue of style to the fact that it is intended as a statement piece.
Wearability: Candidates should give their opinions on the wearability of the piece. Reference should be made to the large scale and the fact that it is likely to be very heavy. Candidates may also discuss other practical considerations, such as the inflexibility of the neckpiece and whether it is likely to be comfortable. Opinion may also be given on health and safety issues relating to wearablility. Candidates may relate the impracticality of the jewellery to its function as a statement piece.

Candidates should be given credit for relevant, well reasoned points made.

(b) This part of the question requires a knowledge and understanding of the work of **two** jewellery designers. The candidates should explain how each designer has created imaginative designs through the discussion of two specific examples. Full answers will make reference to *sources of inspiration, materials and working methods* and demonstrate effective use of terminology.

12. Textile/Fashion Design

(a) Answers should focus on giving opinions on the designer's consideration of the use of materials, aesthetics and target market. Answers should also refer to the hand knitted jacket and sweater having many textures and patterns and by being assembled by sewing different shapes together. The fringed skirt, which has been woven in plaid pattern, has gathers to create the shape. Any reference made to the beauty of the movement and rhythm of these garments will be well rewarded. Opinions on whom the target market for these garments might be should also be offered.

(b) Answers should compare the work of **two** textile/fashion designers. Examples of their work should be discussed referring to the most important features of their style. Answers may focus on two design movements or styles. This perfectly acceptable.

ART AND DESIGN INTERMEDIATE 2 2011

OVERVIEW

The Art and Design Studies Examination Component 2 – Question Paper has been set with the following principles in mind:

1. The examination set for Art and Design Studies at Intermediate 2 level should clearly articulate with the Higher level. The format of the Intermediate 2 examination paper is therefore similar to the Higher paper with respect to the reference materials used and the six headed questions in each of the two sections: Art Studies and Design Studies.

2. Intermediate 2 candidates are required to demonstrate knowledge and understanding of selected aspects of the visual arts and design and to formulate, explain and communicate personal opinions and conclusions. The format of the questions reflects this emphasis. Each question has two equally demanding parts.

   Parts (a) and (b) are designed to test the candidates' ability to respond critically to a range of visual arts imagery and design products and to form and substantiate judgements about identified aspects of art practice and design issues. The questions also require candidates to demonstrate knowledge and understanding gained through their Art and Design Studies as follows:

   Part (a)
   This part of the question requires candidates to give an analytical response to a selected illustration from the supplied reference materials using appropriate terminology and making reference to identified aspects of Art and Design practice. The questions set require candidates to discuss specific art/design issues. While judgement and flexibility should be applied by the marker, candidates who do not address all aspects of the question cannot be awarded full marks.

   Part (b)
   This part of the question requires candidates to make a personal critical response to identified visual elements and art practice in Section 1 of the paper and to identify visual aspects and design issues in Section 2 of the paper. Candidates are expected to substantiate reasons to support judgements and personal opinions expressed in their responses to this part of the question.

3. All questions are of equal demand. The questions should be suitable for candidates with a relatively detailed knowledge as well as those whose knowledge is more wide ranging.

4. Overall, the examination paper makes certain demands on markers, particularly with regard to part (b) of each question. It is possible that candidates will have studied artists and designers of whom little is known to the marker. In such cases, the marker would have to use his or her professional experience and consider how likely it is that an apparently detailed, informative and thoughtful answer is the spontaneous invention of some ill-informed candidate.

   The overriding advice to markers would be to consider if the answer is evidence of any specialist knowledge and understanding of an identifiable area of the visual arts or design. If a candidate who had not followed an Art or Design course or unit of Art and Design Studies and demonstrated no specialist knowledge and understanding could have written the answer, then very little credit could be given.

   It is important to consider, however, that candidates can and will respond with answers, to this part of the question, that contain a depth of knowledge and understanding of their specialist area of the visual arts and design. In these instances, candidates should be well rewarded.

Candidates are expected to demonstrate their knowledge and understanding with reference to specific artworks/designs. Responses which contain only historical and/or biographical information and which do not fully address the question can gain a maximum of only **5 marks**.

At this level, candidates are rewarded for naming their selected artists and designers and the corresponding artworks and designs which they intend to discuss in their answers. A maximum of **1 mark** is available within each part (b) response for this information.

Candidates who discuss only one artist/designer in a part (b) response cannot have fully answered the question set. In this case, a maximum of **7 marks** can be awarded.

5. In Art Studies questions, where the term "artist" is used it should be interpreted in its broadest sense, covering painting, printmaking, photography, sculpture, installation, animation, film and video.

6. Similarly in the Design Studies questions, the term "designer" should be inclusive of any form of design.

Art Studies

1. Portraiture

(a) This question should allow the candidate to describe and give justified reasons for this artist's use of *photographic technique*, and *viewpoint* in creating an interesting portrait.

Candidates may refer to the collaged nature of the work and the disjointed image this creates. The candidate may offer to explore how the artist has taken these images and then selected the composition that we see. Some may wish to offer comment on the shape of the final composition and what has been included by the artist in some of the individual photographs, these points should be well rewarded. Positive and negative justifications on the choice of viewpoint in this work should again be rewarded.

A good answer should include comments, which may attempt to cover the relationship the artist has attempted to make with the viewer about this portrait. Their answer may refer to the artist's relationship with his mother, their visit to this abbey, the choice of day may even be interpreted in some way and all of these should be rewarded.

(b) The candidate in this question should use two examples of portraiture by two artists who they can show a knowledge and understanding of. A very sound response may deal with aspects such as visual elements, likeness, mood, expression, pose chosen and the communication of the character of the sitter.

The candidate should be able to discuss the ways in which the artists have selected and used materials and media. They may also wish to comment on the social aspects of the times that the works were produced in.

2. Figure Composition

(a) This part of the question should provoke a range of valid personal responses about the situation portrayed in this work. Candidates should be rewarded for giving a range of opinions on the success or otherwise of this work.

Candidates may offer some justification as to the use of tone in the work and their feeling on the artist's choice of colour and its impact on the work itself. The title may well be discussed in light of the poses captured by the artist, discussing the variety of figures and their roles in this activity and this should again be well rewarded. Some candidates may speculate on the use of colour and may link it to the conditions of the day, if well made these points should be rewarded fully.

The candidates may discuss the static nature of many of the figures and the frozen action of the players in the game in light of their experiences of a tennis match as a moving image.

A good answer will have the candidate make valid comment with justification on the use of *tone, colour,* and *pose*.

(b) The candidates should attempt to discuss the works of two artists who have worked within the genre of figure composition. A very good response should be able to select two works that typify the artists' use of the subject matter. They may wish to discuss artists that reflect the historical nature of the genre or indeed the contemporary works that can be viewed as figurative today. Opinions that relate to each artist's use of media and visual elements should be rewarded.

3. Still Life

(a) In this question the candidate will be expected to justify opinions made on this artist's choice of *shape, colour* and *pattern.*

Some candidates may refer to the abstracted or indeed Cubist nature of this work in relation to the use of shape and may include some comment the flatness of perspective that occurs. They may discuss the possible relationship these objects have in being grouped together for this painting.

Candidates should be well rewarded for making comments on the colour relationships that they observe occurring in the work. Full marks should be awarded to those that are justified in some manner.

It is expected that candidates will offer some explanation as to the artist's use of pattern, both observed and created in the piece and again this should be fully rewarded.

Candidates are then asked to give their personal opinion of this work and references to elements of position used to justify their opinions should be fully rewarded.

(b) The candidates should show their knowledge and understanding of still-life through the discussion and analysis of two artists and two typical works. A very good response will be one that is structured, to show that there is a comparison and contrast of the works selected, with regards to differing media and methods. The still-life genre is very open and a wide range of approaches studied from the historical to the contemporary will be expected.

4. Natural Environment

(a) All candidates should comment on the construction of each of the identified aspects of the work to gain full marks.

Markers should expect and credit the candidates' initial feelings on how well this hunting scene has been painted for us. Comments on the unusual viewpoint with justifications relating to the mood or atmosphere should be well rewarded.

Candidates may well wish to comment upon the scale and relationship that the figure and the tree has to the works meaning as part of the mood or atmosphere.

The candidates may refer to the natural or even seasonal palette that the artist has chosen. They may also make reference to the use of red to highlight the figure in the work all of these points should be fully rewarded. The candidate may offer some justification to the use of shape with the sprawling and dominant shape of the tree filling the picture and the landscape and the hunter being used in

the spaces created between the trees branches any comment that relates to this should be well rewarded. Candidates comments where justified on the shape that occur in the work should be fully rewarded.

(b) This part of the question is open to a variety of personal responses that include examples taken from a wide range of interpretations to the theme of the natural environment. To gain full marks the candidate should have made some attempt to discuss, with justification, points made on possible sources of individual inspiration for each artist. There should be a feeling that the candidate can justify why these are, for them, good examples of the natural environment. Here it is expected that they may use key elements in this discussion. Any attempt to compare and contrast should be rewarded.

5. Built Environment

(a) In this question the candidate will share their opinions on how well the artist has used the three key elements listed in the question to gain full marks.

Candidates would be expected to respond to this work through the information given in the legend and discuss this work as a painting to gain full marks.

For subject matter, texture and *tone* a good answer should deal with each of these elements in light of the realism of the work. Candidates may wish to offer information about the artist's use of colour in expressing the reflective qualities in the cabina and the range of reds used in the brickwork, these should be rewarded. Comments on the cramped and dingy space for the public phone booth may be offered or the unusual choice of a simple cabina and the urban background it sits in should also be rewarded.

The candidates in the latter part of this question may wish to justify their opinions on the possible location and their thoughts on this approach to the built environment in relation to the legend. They may comment upon the relationship for them of a public phone booth as a source of inspiration for the built environment and may make mention of the lack of these in their own urban environments. Candidates may wish to discuss the artists reasons for painting such an image of a very mundane urban scene and may even make reference to film sets or the fact that it is in New York and their experience of this may be limited to film or television imagery. All of these should be well rewarded.

This work, for some candidates may elicit some negative responses; these should be rewarded where they are justified.

(b) Candidates should demonstrate knowledge and understanding of two artists who use the built environment. They should give personal opinions of the artists' works that they have selected to discuss. Any points where the subject is discussed in a fashion that compares and contrasts should assist in gaining full marks.

Those candidates that demonstrate an understanding of the selected artists' methods and or approaches should be well rewarded. To gain full marks they should have attempted to share their opinion of the success of the works.

6. Fantasy and Imagination

(a) This part of the question will ask the candidate to state opinions as to what kind of atmosphere has been created by the artist. Candidates who use a variety of descriptions with justifications should be well rewarded.

The candidate should be rewarded for justification on the points asked for but may wish to add other key elements. The additional points made can be rewarded as part of the comments for the atmosphere, so long as the candidate has answered the question in relation to the use of *colour*, *pattern* and *imagery*.

For Imagery candidates may relate to the floating figures and may make reference to these as angels as well as perhaps identifying the central figure as the Saint. It should be noted that account be taken of the candidates coming from different cultural and religious viewpoints with this image, all relevant points made and justified should be rewarded. Reference may also be made to the figures and birds breaking out onto the decorative border that Duncan has painted, again this should be rewarded if justified.

(b) This part of the question will allow candidates the opportunity to show their knowledge and understanding of the works of two artists they know well who are within the realms of the theme of fantasy and imagination. You should expect well-substantiated opinions of the typical works that they will compare and contrast for full marks.

The candidates may wish to cover the areas of working methods, media used to cover the response on approaches used by each artist.

The answer should contain some form of preference to a work studied and attempt to justify their choice or preference.

Design Studies

7. Graphic Design

(a) The answer should focus on comparisons with contemporary magazine cover design. Candidates are directed to refer to imagery, lettering and layout. Comparisons about imagery may involve discussion about the hand drawn nature of the illustration in contrast with today's photographic approaches. The subject matter in the illustration may also elicit some comment along with the stylisation of the trees and plants. The monochromatic colour scheme could also be compared with more colourful contemporary examples. Some candidates may demonstrate knowledge about the printmaking processes which may have been used to create the imagery in this historical example and the photographic and computer generated graphics of today.

Candidates should comment on the lettering and compare this with contemporary styles. The use of different fonts may be noted. The placement of the lettering within the panel and the 'banners' should be discussed when commenting on the layout. Answers should not merely contain description and candidates will have plenty of scope to give their own personal opinion on how the design compares with today's magazine covers.

Well justified points which are relevant to the question should be awarded marks.

(b) This question requires candidates to discuss two graphic designs by two different designers. They should compare how successfully the examples achieve visual impact and communication with a target audience. Good answers will demonstrate a sound knowledge and understanding of issues relating to graphic design.

8. Product Design

(a) Candidates are asked to respond to how well the designer has considered fitness for purpose and style. They are also instructed to speculate on which target market would have found it appealing. To assist in forming opinions, they are told that the car is small and low cost.

A number of factors contribute to fitness for purpose and candidates may discuss; economy, the number of passengers which could be carried, as well as ergonomic and anthropometric considerations. Comments can be positive or negative.

In discussing style, the appearance of the car should be considered. Candidates may be familiar with the contemporary version and may comment on the fact that the design could be considered a 'classic' which has endured.

Opinion should be given on target market. The car had popular appeal, so this may range from families to young, first time drivers. Comments may be related to cost. As long as points are well justified, they should be rewarded.

(b) Candidates should select two products by two different designers and identify the key design issues considered. They are asked to discuss each designer's approach to creating a successful product.

The question allows candidates to comment on design issues particularly relevant to their chosen designers and to show their knowledge and understanding of this area.

9. Interior Design

(a) Candidates should give their opinion on how well the designers have created this interior for a high street store. They should give their views on the success of the use of space and style and how these contribute to its consumer appeal.

In commenting on use of space, candidates may discuss the division of the space into different areas and how the designers have created space around the displays to allow flow of traffic. The use of various fixtures and fittings for hanging garments and displaying merchandise may be noted and discussed.

Candidates should attempt to describe the style created and may make reference to colour schemes, signage and use of mannequins.

As many candidates will be familiar with this type of store, they may conclude that it appeals to young consumers, but any well reasoned opinions should be awarded marks.

(b) Candidates are directed to select two interiors by two different designers. They should compare the methods used to create effective and attractive interior spaces. The question allows candidates to demonstrate their knowledge and understanding of interior design and to comment specifically on functional and aesthetic issues.

10. Environmental/Architectural Design

(a) This question requires candidates to give their opinion on the design of this building, referring to structure and use of materials. They are also asked to consider the designer's source of inspiration.

The unusual structure of the building should be discussed. Some candidates may comment on the complexity of the form and how the building integrates with the landscape.

Information is given on the materials used to allow candidates to make informed opinions. The contrast of the different materials, as well as their suitability, will provide scope for discussion.

Various sources of inspiration could be suggested. Some may realise that the location has influenced the structure, particularly the design windows, which make the most of the panoramic views.

Candidates are told the purpose of the building and may refer to this in their answers.

Well justified opinions relevant to the questions should gain marks.

(b) Candidates are asked to compare two successful examples of environmental/architectural design by two different designers with reference to important design issues. This allows candidates to focus on issues which are particularly relevant to their chosen examples and to demonstrate their knowledge and understanding of this area of design. Good responses will identify and discuss issues which are key to the success of the designs.

11. Jewellery Design

(a) Candidates are informed that the designer's source of inspiration is to do with the human body and are asked to give their opinion on this. When discussing style, good responses will discuss the designer's particular interpretation of this theme. Information is given on materials and there may be discussion of how the designer has formed these materials to create the pieces and the repetition of the circle as a motif. The colour scheme and the use of red as an accent colour should be noted.

Candidates should also comment on who might find these pieces attractive to buy. This will direct the candidates to speculate on the designer's target market. Any opinions which are well justified and relevant should be rewarded.

(b) This question requires candidates to select two examples of jewellery by two different designers. They are directed to compare the designers' influences and the techniques used to make visually appealing designs. This gives candidates the opportunity to demonstrate their knowledge and understanding of jewellery design issues. Good answers should address all aspects of the question.

12. Textile/Fashion Design

(a) This question asks candidates to consider how well the designer has created shoes which make a fashion statement. They should refer to form and practicality and give their opinion on who might have worn these shoes.

An attempt should be made to describe the dramatic form of the shoe with its platform sole, and how this 'over the top' design could be considered a fashion statement. The use of colour to accentuate the form may elicit comment.

When discussing issues of practicality, it will probably be noted that this is not an everyday shoe but a high fashion item, where practical issues are secondary to style.

Some comment may be made on how the shoe fastens and how difficult it may be to walk in. Health and Safety could be discussed.

Candidates will probably conclude that these shoes would have been worn by very fashion conscious individuals. They may comment on the typical personality of the wearer and on what occasions the shoes might be worn. They may be surprised at the date of production and relate the shoe to similar contemporary examples.

Positive and negative opinions may be given as long as statement are justified and relate to question.

(b) Answers should identify two examples of textiles/fashion design by two different designers. The appeal to specific target markets should be discussed with reference to style and use of materials. Candidates should demonstrate a knowledge and understanding of these issues in relation to textile/fashion design. Thorough responses will discuss all aspects of the question.

Hey! I've done it

BrightRED
PUBLISHING

© 2011 SQA/Bright Red Publishing Ltd, All Rights Reserved
Published by Bright Red Publishing Ltd, 6 Stafford Street, Edinburgh, EH3 7AU
Tel: 0131 220 5804, Fax: 0131 220 6710, enquiries: sales@brightredpublishing.co.uk,
www.brightredpublishing.co.uk

Official SQA answers to 978-1-84948-193-9
2008-2011